GREATEST
RUGBY UNION
PLAYERS OF ALL TIME

IN ASSOCIATION WITH
TIMPSON

3011813307317 5

D0928510

GREATEST
RUGBY UNION
PLAYERS OF ALL TIME

STEVEN WHITE

Published in the UK in 2015 by
Icon Books Ltd, Omnibus Business Centre,
39–41 North Road, London N7 9DP
email: info@iconbooks.com
www.iconbooks.com

Sold in the UK, Europe and Asia
by Faber & Faber Ltd, Bloomsbury House,
74–77 Great Russell Street,
London WC1B 3DA or their agents

Distributed in the UK, Europe and Asia
by TBS Ltd, TBS Distribution Centre, Colchester Road,
Frating Green, Colchester CO7 7DW

Distributed in Australia and New Zealand
by Allen & Unwin Pty Ltd,
PO Box 8500, 83 Alexander Street,
Crows Nest, NSW 2065

Distributed in South Africa by
Jonathan Ball, Office B4, The District,
41 Sir Lowry Road, Woodstock 7925

Distributed in India by Penguin Books India,
7th Floor, Infinity Tower – C, DLF Cyber City,
Gurgaon 122002, Haryana

Distributed in Canada by Publishers Group Canada,
76 Stafford Street, Unit 300
Toronto, Ontario M6J 2S1

ISBN 978-178578-026-4

CONTENTS

INTRODUCTION

S electing the 50 greatest rugby union players of all time has been an incredible task. There has been a lot of time spent watching old footage, which has been immensely enjoyable, and a lot of time too spent arranging and rearranging the order until I was happy that I had a 50 that represented the very pinnacle of the sport. It has been an honour, although inevitably it has also involved some painful decisions. The game has seen far more than 50 greats and there have been some astonishing players whose stories I have not had room to tell.

By far the most difficult consideration when compiling this list was attempting to analyse individuals in this most team-based of sports. A player is only ever as good in defence as the man outside him. And what's the use of a scrum-half with incredible distribution if the fly-half's positioning is below par? Almost all of the players included here had the fortune to play alongside some wonderful players.

Since the first international game in 1871, the sport of rugby union has gone through so many changes that it is virtually unrecognisable from the game that is played today. There were some phenomenally important players from those early days; the tales of the New Zealand Originals and the Invincibles tour are legendary and their influence is still felt today. However, the changes in the laws and playing styles over time make it even more of a curious challenge to compare and contrast abilities.

For instance, I have not included a single full-back who played before the rule change in 1963 to prevent teams kicking straight to touch from anywhere on the pitch. Before then, the job of the full-back was almost entirely defensive and based on kicking. Since that law change we've seen full-back become one of the most important (and exciting) positions on the pitch.

Another problem I faced is that you are not always comparing like with like. When you place two players side by side and one is a prop and the other a winger, how do you decide who is better? You have to look beyond the statistics, beyond the points scored and competitions won (although it goes without saying that the greatest players are more likely to be on the winning side). I chose to pore over old footage, re-watching classic games and focusing on individuals to try to see who had consistently had a great impact on the game.

This approach has its limitations, given the game's long history and the many legendary players for whom extensive footage does not exist. Expert testimonies, such as Gareth Edwards' *100 Great Rugby Players* (in which he did not feel the need to rank them in anything other than alphabetical order), have proved invaluable for filling in the gaps.

Still, one has to be mindful of the nostalgia that surrounds some of those players of yesteryear. This is not a history of the sport, and there would be a different bias if we were to include players for their historical significance or for the romance attached to their stories. I have tried to set aside nostalgia and judge each player on their contributions on the pitch, and as such it would have been difficult to leave out someone like Shane Williams for Gwyn Nicholls, or to remove Sean Fitzpatrick in order to make room for Dave Gallaher.

I have tried to eliminate bias (and not simply select the entirety of the 2003 England World Cup-winning team) and I have found that re-watching footage with a different eye has resulted in certain trends. The first is a heavy Kiwi representation, and I doubt that people will find that too contentious. As the All Blacks will be the first to point out, all things considered, the New Zealand rugby union team are the greatest sporting team in history. And while overall the most successful nations have a nice representation, this list can't escape the dominance of the All Blacks.

The other trend that has emerged in this selection is perhaps more controversial. As alluded to above, some undoubtedly legendary figures have been omitted where I felt that their legend owed more to their story than to their playing ability. I have attempted to remove the rose-tinted glasses of nostalgia and the end result is a selection of players which may lead to mass outrage and tables overturned by old boys in clubhouses across the world at the sheer quantity of professional-era players. I stand by each and every selection. I think that although some may argue that the romance of the sport dwindled as money rolled in and the importance of winning became tied up with marketing opportunities and all-important sponsors, ultimately, the competition grew fiercer and it gave an opportunity for the real talent to go out on to the pitch and express itself to a greater audience.

But for all my attempts at reason and objectivity, ultimately, the romance of the sport has played its part in every one of these selections. The little guy, the smart guy, the guy built like an outhouse with the surprising kicking ability. The fire, the passion, the leadership. Statistics may play a part, but every single one of these 50 players has or had something unquantifiable, something that meant every time they laced up their boots and pulled on their jersey they had the power to raise the hairs on the back of your neck and make this most special of sports even more magical.

THE 50 GREATEST RUGBY UNION PLAYERS

50. GRANT FOX

Fly-half, New Zealand 1984–93

This World Cup-winning fly-half may not have been the greatest natural ball-carrier New Zealand have ever had in this position, but he was a pivotal player in one of many periods of dominance the All Blacks have held over world rugby.

A master in the art of goal-kicking, indeed, Fox was a real innovator. He was one of the first players to popularise the leaning forward of the ball on the tee and the first to have a real recognisable routine, so common in the kickers of today. His calm backward and side-steps, accompanied by heavy exhaling as he calmed himself before striking, became a familiar sight throughout the late 1980s and early '90s.

He was perhaps not one for the romantics; Fox was not a flair player, he did not display huge amounts of imagination and was rarely found dashing through the lines – but he did score an astronomical amount of points. Indeed, he would kick so many penalties and conversions that New Zealand would find themselves dominating the scoreboard, even without having to perform particularly well. Often all it would take was for the All Blacks to keep their discipline and wait for the penalties – and therefore the points – to pile up.

Despite him immediately scoring huge points totals following his test debut in 1985, Fox did not have a secure place in the side, facing competition from the likes of Wayne Smith and Frano Botica. In 1986, he was part of the widely

condemned New Zealand Cavaliers tour of South Africa. Fox was banned for three tests, allowing the young Botica into the side. It caused a selection headache, Botica initiated lovely free-flowing attacks, he was a powerful runner and overall a more creative outside half. All instincts led to Botica's selection, but the fact remained that the All Blacks were simply more likely to win with Grant Fox in the side.

By the time the inaugural World Cup rolled around in 1987, Fox was the undisputed fly-half of choice. New Zealand won the tournament quite comfortably, with a team that included other great players such as Sean Fitzpatrick and Michael Jones. Fox played a huge part in that victory, finishing the tournament as top scorer with an immense 126 points, which remains a record for the most points any single player has ever scored at a World Cup. With their remorseless style, New Zealand were able to take every single game away from their opposition quite quickly and won every game by a comfortable margin of at least twenty points.

This was perfectionism, even before the days of professionalism. Fox was passionate about his analysis and training. His dedication to winning was single-minded and set the standard for the days of crafted, well-drilled players. There was a languid, self-assured style to Fox's play that controlled the All Blacks back line from '87 through to '93. Fox's mood often typified the performance the entire side displayed and so much rested on him. When the fly-half was calm and collected, New Zealand would stroll to victory, but on the rare occasion that the Kiwis suffered a defeat, Fox's perfectionism bubbled over into visible annoyance and there was no recovery.

Fox remained a fixture in the All Blacks back line-up until the winning series against the British & Irish Lions in 1993 when he dramatically scored a match-winning kick in the first test in the dying moments, ending his career at the end of that international season.

After Fox's retirement, the All Blacks really struggled to find a replacement. Many were tried and rejected, but 1995 saw the emergence of another outstanding goal-kicker in Andrew Mehrtens, who was Fox's true successor.

Though Mehrtens eventually exceeded many of Fox's scoring records, it was done through echoing and mimicking the style of play that Fox introduced. In 78 matches for the All Blacks Fox scored 1,067 points and only 1 try (his lack of try scoring was the source of many jokes from both the media and teammates). But for good or ill, Fox changed the way the game was played forever.

49. OS DU RANDT

Prop, South Africa 1994–2000, 2004–07

Known for his powerful scrummaging and indomitable work rate, Jacobus du Randt is one of the most revered prop forwards the game has ever seen and a true South African hero. Nicknamed 'Ox' ('Os' in Afrikaans), the iconic prop is the only South African to have won two World Cups, with three years out of the game in between.

Du Randt suffered a devastating injury when in peak form in 2000 and believed his career to be over after being sidelined for three years. He battled back in one of the most astonishing comebacks in rugby history to reclaim a place in the World Cup squad in 2007, twelve years after South Africa's inaugural success in the competition.

Making his debut against Argentina in 1994, Randt quickly cemented his position as the first-choice loosehead prop. Du Randt entered the 1995 World Cup in the front row of a solid Bok scrum. He was yet to lose an international test and his naivety perhaps proved useful as he entered every scrum like he believed he was invincible. Nowhere was this more evident than in the semi-final against a tough France side on a sodden pitch. The Springboks had to hold on in the final moments of the game under intense pressure as they faced a series of five-metre scrums, with du Randt holding his own to become the real unsung hero of the tournament.

The scrum was also to play a pivotal role in the final against New Zealand. The tactics employed by the Springboks involved a tight physical game, as they were desperate to shut out Jonah Lomu. The most crucial plays of the day came out of the scrum and du Randt held his nerve for the scrimmage in the dying seconds of the game, allowing his team the platform to score the decisive drop-goal.

In the intermediary years between World Cup successes, du Randt made his name as the best and most dependable prop forward in the world, entering the 1999 World Cup at the top of his game. While the Springboks were ultimately defeated in the semi-final by eventual winners Australia, Os du Randt was one of the best players of the tournament again. His status as the best remained until a chronic knee injury in 2000 kept him on the sideline for three years with his future in the game coming under threat.

After a slow recovery, he was coaxed out of retirement and convinced to play for former club Free State Cheetahs. Things went well for his provincial side, and although he had never intended to play for South Africa again, he was swayed to make himself available for international selection in 2004.

Things did not go entirely to plan and initially it did not look like a fairy-tale comeback for du Randt as high-profile defeats to both Australia and New Zealand in the Tri-Nations (although the Springboks still managed to scrape the championship title) were followed by touring side losses to Ireland and England in the autumn internationals that same year. The England game in particular exposed some weakness in the Springbok pack, with the scrummaging coming under scrutiny as they were turned over repeatedly in this area. Nevertheless du Randt worked hard to retain his place for an unforeseen three years up to and including the 2007 World Cup. Here is where the second part of the du Randt story really stands out.

Aged 36, du Randt was named man of the match in the semi-final victory over Argentina. Los Pumas had surprised many by reaching the semis, and had done so through expert scrummaging and a tight pack. Du Randt used all of his experience to pick their game plan apart in a tough contest. Os was in inspired form for the Bokke and played the full 80 minutes of their final victory over England, not looking like a player ready to retire. Not content with holding down the scrum and securing the breakdown, du Randt made one incisive run in particular where he looked in his prime. South Africa won the 2007 World Cup by virtue of their superior and mighty pack, the experience of du Randt proving invaluable to his side as well as a romantic story to endear himself to the fans, carving out a special place in Springbok legend.

48. FRANK BUNCE

Centre, Western Samoa 1991, New Zealand 1992–97

Frank Bunce managed a surprising 55 caps for the All Blacks despite being something of a late bloomer, not making his debut until he was 30. He may have been a late arrival to the international rugby scene, but his brutal and unforgiving presence in New Zealand's midfield provided some much-needed stability through the 1990s.

What made this granite-like centre even more unusual is that, like Michael Jones, he was poached after making his initial appearances for Western Samoa. The Samoans were the surprise package of the 1991 Rugby World Cup, with Bunce at the heart of the side, before he switched his allegiance to play for the country of his birth.

Bunce's hard-working, honest approach made him an effective centre and counterbalance to his much more unpredictable Wallabies opposite number Tim Horan. They often brought out the best in each other, making their individual contests one of the highlights of the Bledisloe Cup during the mid-'90s. Bunce provided the power to complement his technically impressive side. In defence, there were few as solid and technically adept, hitting with a real crunch, often relieving his side and even turning over the ball with his work at the breakdown; it was such that a back-rower would have been proud.

That said, Bunce was not simply a lump, throwing himself at the opposition. His power and pace made him a dangerous runner and prolific try scorer. It seems a straightforward approach, but Bunce was at his most dangerous towards the end of a match, when any lapse in concentration or tiring legs were exposed by the superior stamina of the machine-like midfielder as he pounced and broke the defensive line time and time again.

Perhaps not blessed with the natural gifts of Horan or Philippe Sella, Bunce made up for it with graft and hard work. Frank Bunce spent the majority of his career at Auckland, although for many years was not a first-choice player. It was only when he moved to North Harbour in 1991 that he gained enough first-team experience to warrant inclusion in the budding Western Samoa side that sparked a late renaissance of his stalled career. Western Samoa surprised everyone by defeating Wales and Argentina to make the knockout stages of the World Cup, with Bunce's blistering physicality the cornerstone of their success. An offer to play for the All Blacks was too good to refuse and Bunce linked up with North Harbour teammate Walter Little in the midfield to form a terrifying partnership.

Once given the opportunity, Bunce grabbed it with both hands and only missed one test in the next five years, even appearing at the first Sevens World Cup in 1993. Bunce used his strength selflessly in the field, using his upper body strength to offload and bring his outside centre or winger into play to great effect. Such was his relentless approach that he even managed twenty test tries himself. His impact was never more keenly felt than in the 1995 Rugby World Cup, where his diversionary tactics were used to unleash Jonah Lomu on the unsuspecting home nations.

From the moment he made his belated international debut, Frank Bunce persistently defied expectations to continue at the top level, playing his last game for New Zealand in 1997, just before his 36th birthday, a draw at Twickenham ending an eleven-game winning streak.

47. BRYAN HABANA

Wing, South Africa 2004–

South Africa's World Cup victory in 1995 had a huge impact not only on the sport, but on the political landscape of a nation. It also left a huge impression on a future star. Aged twelve, Bryan Habana was in the stands as he watched his emerging rainbow nation become champions in a sport that was relatively new to him (having attended a school that prioritised soccer). Habana left the stadium that day with a t-shirt printed with a photo of his own smiling face in the centre with the inscription 'I'm the Bokke's greatest supporter'. Habana waited after the game to get the autographs of both the All Blacks and Springbok teams, and his face ended up surrounded by the signatures of his new heroes.

Twelve years later and Bryan Habana was lifting the Webb Ellis trophy after finishing the tournament as the top try scorer, and later that year was honoured as the greatest player in the world with the award of the 2007 IRB Player of the Year trophy.

Habana is someone who seemed destined to become a world great right from the start. A natural rugby player, he made his Springboks debut as a replacement against England on 20 November 2004, scoring a try with his first touch of the ball.

Habana quickly established himself as indispensible for the Springboks, starting every single test in 2005, scoring twelve tries in twelve tests to earn him a first nomination for that IRB World Player of the Year award. The emergence of their new superstar came at just the right time for South Africa who had struggled to emulate their success in the years following the 1995 World Cup and had lacked a truly world-class winger, with their biggest try-scoring threat in recent years having come from the by-now-retired captain and scrum-half Joost van der Westhuizen. Habana provided something that South Africa had been lacking: width. His two long-range tries against Australia in the summer of 2005 helped the Springboks win their first Tri-Nations match overseas for seven years.

Habana, who has been clocked at 10.2 seconds running the 100 metres, made headlines around the world in 2007 by racing a cheetah to raise awareness to the plight of the near-extinct animal. Now, it's not a huge surprise to learn that Habana did not win that race, even with a 35-yard head start. But it was close, and as a publicity stunt for a charity, as much as showcasing the incredible speed of one of the fastest men in the world, it highlighted Habana's popularity and charisma outside of the world of rugby.

Bryan Habana entered the 2007 Rugby World Cup as an already established superstar but left as one of the true greats, having proven himself on the world stage and, with a total of eight tries, having managed to equal Jonah Lomu's record for tries in one tournament. Following the World Cup victory, South Africa's domination quickly foundered; a change in playing style did not suit Habana, who failed to make any impact at all during 2008. An expansive style did not suit any of the back line but as the finisher, the superstar and the furthest exposed on the wing, Habana took more than his fair share of the blame. He rose to the challenge of his critics, revaluated his playing style and in the 2009 season was a pure defensive rock. He gained some weight and really worked on the perceived weaker aspects of his game, and he

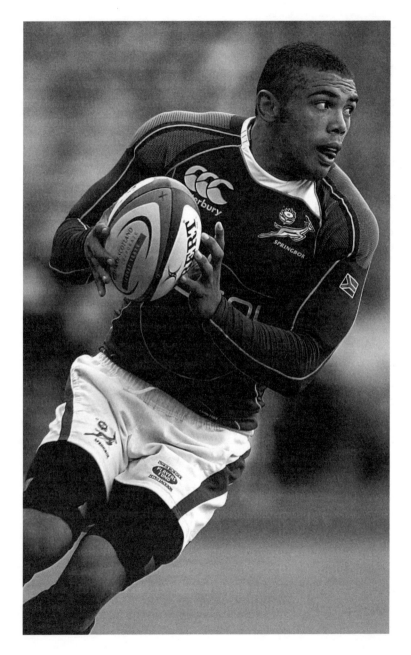

managed to do this without sacrificing his killer try-scoring instincts. That year Habana was selected in the South Africa side to play the British & Irish Lions and was dependable in defence, as well as scoring a memorable try in the second test, as the Springboks won the series.

But Habana is more than just speed and a strong tackle. With ball in hand, his superior upper body strength in the tackle often gains crucial yards as he drives the defender back and uses his power to give his pack enough time to secure the breakdown, even as he often finds himself isolated by sheer speed. This strength, accompanied by his sharp awareness, means that when a teammate can keep up, Habana can be very dangerous in the offload.

Using his pace, Habana can also do the undervalued donkey work, the chasing of kicks that can really put a team under pressure, something not enough of the speedy wingers do consistently at the top level. He will control his run with unbelievable accuracy, leaving him to arrive at precisely the time to hammer his opponent down to the ground. He played as both scrum-half and centre throughout junior rugby before settling to the wing. This time spent at half-back and in the midfield gave Habana extra dimensions to his game; his handling and positional awareness are superior to those of most wingers and are used ruthlessly to exploit the opposition in their own 22.

The 2015 Rugby World Cup saw a slightly different side to Habana, as his South Africa side struggled slightly and lost many of its most experienced players to injury. As well as the physical knocks, they suffered humiliation at the hands of the excellent Japanese in their opening game and Habana played like a man with something to prove for the rest of the tournament. With much of the media focusing on another Jonah Lomu record – his overall tally of fifteen World Cup tries – and Habana's expected retirement, the pressure was on, and sometimes it showed. On the occasions where he was allowed to enjoy his rugby, he propelled South Africa into the semi-finals. But a tough clash with the incomparable All Blacks was too much for the Springboks, resulting in a narrow defeat, with Habana showing his frustration and marching to the sin bin following a cynical challenge at the breakdown. Consignment to the periphery in the third-place play-off was an unfortunate way for Habana to exit what was surely his final World Cup. With the world waiting for the final, Habana spent the match trying to put on a show for the spectators and attempting to score the one try that would have broken Lomu's record. Ultimately, he failed.

Even taking all this into account, Habana is simply one of the greatest finishers the game has ever seen. Whether rubbing salt in the wounds of the opposing fans or delighting his own supporters, Habana always plays, and scores, with a smile on his face.

46. SYD MILLAR

Prop, Ireland 1958–70

Syd Millar may well be more remembered for his coaching and his time as chairman of the IRB than for his playing days. But before all of that, the former prop was a formidable player for both Ireland and the British & Irish Lions throughout the 1960s.

If one man encapsulates the spirit, tradition and sense of special occasion that defines the British & Irish Lions, then

it's Syd Millar. He completed three tours as a player before coaching the famous 1974 tour of South Africa and even returned to manage the side against the Springboks in 1980.

This desire to compete and to win that he instilled into the later tours heralded back to his playing career; he would do everything it took to win. Reportedly, Millar began his career playing at fly-half in his schoolboy days, and as a sixteen-stone prop forward, those handling skills made him a rare and great asset for Ballymena and Ireland.

An incredibly versatile player, he played both loosehead and tighthead for the Lions over the years, and was the most-used prop in the 1962 tour, playing in 16 of the 24 matches, offering more to the game than sheer size and scrummaging. Although the Lions ultimately lost that tour 3-0, Syd Millar fared well against his opposition.

Despite this, however, Millar was not selected for the 1966 Lions tour to Australia and New Zealand. It is a testament to his character that in the following years he fought his way back into contention for one final tour in 1968, once again to South Africa. Millar was tough and being dropped did not dent his confidence, only inspired him to improve himself.

Even today, being a tight forward requires a lot of resilience in the face of off-the-ball incidents; the front row of the scrum is a hotbed for cheap shots that players love to use to wind up and grind down their opponents. It was even worse in the '60s. With no television crews, no citations and only one referee to spot the incidents, so many went under the radar, even by the crowd. But Millar was a proud player who rarely bit back – even when literally bitten. With cheap shots flying and teeth sinking, it was lucky that the Ireland captain of the time, Bill Mulcahy, was a trainee doctor. With no replacements available, it was not uncommon for

Mulcahy himself to treat Millar on the side of the pitch before returning to the field.

This experience inevitably helped Millar become an expert on a most physical national side: South Africa. He was involved in four successive tours there (two as a player, one as a coach and then finally as a manager in 1980) with varying degrees of success. He used his expertise to help the Lions prepare for the physicality of the immortal 1974 tour.

As a player, his finest moment for the Lions didn't come against the Springboks but right at the start of his career, against Australia. Although that same tour saw two test match losses against New Zealand, Millar was a key player in the two victories over Australia and he rates that '59 side as the best he ever played in.

Even after he was no longer Lions coach, his insatiable appetite for rugby saw him become chairman of the IRU in 1995, then chairman of the IRB from 2003 to 2007. His contribution to the game of rugby both on and off the pitch is incomparable.

45. KEN CATCHPOLE

Scrum-half, Australia 1961–68

Although hailing from an Aussie Rules-playing family, Ken Catchpole was one of the most recognisable and fondly remembered rugby union players ever to captain the Wallabies.

There are relatively few now who will remember seeing Ken Catchpole in his glory days, but his image is instantly

recognisable. A distinguishing stance with his eyes firmly on the receiver, his posture an indication of the power behind the pass, whether that was with a planted back foot or from a diving pass.

Much like the future captain George Gregan, Catchpole was small, but mighty. He was fast and tough, a truly sturdy player. His endurance often saw him the liveliest player on the pitch in the final minutes of the game, making last-ditch tackles and stealing ball from the opposition breakdown right to the final whistle. Catchpole was a great all-round scrum-half; it's not often a half-back can combine consistent distribution with defensive dependency as well as a flair to find the galvanising run in broken field, but Catchpole in his prime displayed all of these qualities.

Despite making his debut against Fiji in 1961, aged 21 – bizarrely starting as captain – it took Catchpole two years to establish himself as Australia's starting number nine. Crucially, Phil Hawthorne made his debut aged eighteen in 1962 and Catchpole's combination with this incredibly talented fly-half was the basis for many historic Wallabies victories during the 1960s.

In stark contrast to many hard-hitting and aggressive back lines of the time, Catchpole and Hawthorne set about carving up defences with an elegance that took most sides by surprise. The basis for this successful strategy lay with Ken's impeccable passing and tactical leadership.

The records came tumbling and history books were rewritten almost immediately as Ken Catchpole was named captain for the South African tour of 1963. It was during this tour that the Wallabies became the first team ever to visit and defeat the Springboks in successive tests.

It was on the 1966/67 tour to Great Britain that Catchpole announced himself to an unsuspecting set of home nations and cemented his legendary status. Australia not only achieved a first ever victory over Wales but also registered a record victory against England at Twickenham. The 23 points scored (Catchpole contributing a try) was the most that England had ever conceded in 'the fortress' since the first test there in 1910. Although not always known for their generosity, the English press and key commentators recognised Catchpole as the greatest half-back the world had ever known.

Catchpole was a nightmare for the opposition back rows during these matches. The northern hemisphere sides were not used to playing against such an opportunistic scrum-half who, standing at only five foot five, was constantly biting around at the breakdown, holding an unexpectedly strong base; one who marshalled his own forwards, snapped at their heels and sent the ball out with lightning pace. What really made life difficult for the opposition back row was when he stood on the opposite side of the ball to his outside half, no matter the distance that the pass needed to be, something which future scrum-halves would aspire to.

Catchpole was generations ahead of his time with a graceful and insightful manner of play. The sign of a great scrum-half is the distribution of ball with pace and timing that can gives the outside half precious extra seconds to coordinate the attack. Catchpole did this and then some. The Wallabies are famed even now for open, running rugby. Perhaps their squad of the 1980s with Mark Ella and David Campese illustrated this to a wider audience, but certainly the short, sharp passes of Catchpole and Hawthorne went against the thinking of the time and laid the foundations for the success of the future. Their approach was not uniformly successful – the game immediately preceding the famous Twickenham victory in 1967 saw Australia lose to Scotland.

But with their numerous other victories, Catchpole and his Australian side showed the world that there were many ways to run a back line and opened up a whole new set of tactics, shaping the modern game.

Perhaps with a longer career, Catchpole could have achieved even more, but his career was ended in 1968 by Colin 'Pinetree' Meads. In one of his less honourable moments, Pinetree pulled on Catchpole's leg when his body was trapped in a ruck, tearing his hamstring. It was a horrific injury from which he never recovered and Ken Catchpole retired aged 28. Hawthorne switched to rugby league the same year Catchpole retired, becoming a dual-code international and enjoying great success.

Catchpole left an enduring legacy and the medal that is awarded annually to the best club player in New South Wales bears his name. This is just one of the ways in which Catchpole casts his shadow over the Wallabies' proud tradition of cutting back lines. His style of play laid the foundations for generations to come.

44. VICTOR MATFIELD

Lock, South Africa 2000–11, 2014–15

Victor Matfield is yet another South African forward who couldn't resist this wonderful sport and simply could not stay retired, making a comeback to rival that of his compatriot Os du Randt, yet without quite the fairy-tale ending.

Making his debut at the start of the 21st century, when South African rugby was full of superstars such as John Smit,

Joost van der Westhuizen and Schalk Burger, Matfield was to emerge as the talisman for his side throughout the decade to come. An immense physical presence and an impressive specimen of athletic dominance, he would go on to win every honour available in world rugby while personifying the shuddering intimidation of a Springbok.

From a technical perspective, Matfield is quite possibly the best lineout performer the game has ever seen. As rugby has progressed and tidied up the area of the lineout and the game has become more streamlined in this area, to have a player like Matfield who would not only dominate the skies physically, but who had the canny ability to steal a lineout through sheer intelligence, was to become of utmost importance to South Africa.

Indeed, Matfield's constant supply of ball was to become a real cornerstone of their tactics in the Springboks' World Cup triumph in 2007. Man of the match in the final, as well as overall player of the tournament, Victor Matfield was able to show his versatility in an otherwise unexciting final that South Africa dominated over a limp England. Not content with his skills at the lineout, in the scrum and at the breakdown, Matfield demonstrated his superb ball-playing skills, delivering a perfect touch-finding kick that any outside half would have been proud of.

Pace is not usually the attribute most closely associated with a second-row forward, but Matfield's sprint could almost match that of teammate Bryan Habana. He was not only a fast and strong runner, but an intelligent one too. The fantastic rugby brain Matfield possessed was one of completeness; vision in the lineout was not the limit of his skills, although he remained the undisputed master of that area of the game.

Following the World Cup victory, 2009 in particular was a

successful year for Matfield, as he played a pivotal role in a series victory over the British & Irish Lions as well as winning his second Tri-Nations title with South Africa, claiming a hat-trick of victories over the All Blacks along the way.

Matfield retired in 2011, becoming a TV pundit in South Africa, commentating on Super Rugby, as well as remaining as forwards coach at his former club the Bulls. He would still have been remembered fondly as one of the greatest Springboks ever, even before reversing his retirement to make a spectacular comeback.

Victor Matfield was coaxed out of retirement to play for the Bulls in 2014; the temptation to play first-class rugby was just too great for a man who never strayed too far from the action and was still in great physical fitness. He impressed in the following Super Rugby season and was a surprise selection in South Africa's 2015 World Cup squad. Since Matfield's retirement, many of South Africa's weaknesses had stemmed from poor lineouts and kick-offs, both strengths of Matfield; they had never really been able to replace him.

Following the incomparable upset in the opening game at the hands of the Brave Blossoms, Matfield and his captain Jean de Villiers received a stern dressing-down for not following coach Heyneke Meyer's instructions or game plan. They were reportedly given twenty minutes to prove themselves in the Samoa game and threatened with replacement thereafter. This bold tactic worked as motivation and de Villiers and Matfield gave inspired performances to lift their devastated and shocked squad. Further distress was to be placed upon the squad however, when de Villiers broke his jaw and subsequently retired from the game, leaving Matfield as captain. It was particularly heartbreaking for de Villiers who had already missed two World Cup campaigns due to injury. Matfield and Meyer did not allow their side to lose heart and the forward's experience in the dressing room proved invaluable.

Matfield picked up a niggle himself and was unable to play in the comprehensive victories over Scotland and the USA, with the young Lood de Jager making some breakthrough performances under the veteran's tutelage. Victor Matfield recovered from his injury to make a replacement appearance in the semi-final against the superlative All Blacks in what was to prove a tight and physical affair. His heroics in the rain were not enough to defeat New Zealand, but his performance was strong enough for this legendary figure to retire in style, again.

43. JOHN SMIT

Hooker, South Africa 2000–11

John Smit was the motivating and inspiring leader who lifted the World Cup with the Springboks in 2007, guiding them through their greatest period of the professional era.

South Africa's most-capped captain was incredibly consistent throughout his career and was ever-present as the anchor of the Springbok pack. His career started with a bang and Smit looked the complete package right from his debut in 2000, impressing in a victory against Argentina.

The start to his career was not to be as straightforward as that, however, as a recurring shoulder injury kept him from the international scene for eighteen months. Smit then worked hard to prove himself fit for the Sharks and had to fight his way back into the squad in time for the 2003 World

Cup, where despite a modest showing by South Africa, Smit performed well as a great leader on the pitch.

In early 2004, the new Springboks coach Jake White handed Smit the captaincy. Finding immediate success, Smit and White led South Africa to their first Tri-Nations crown that year, their first since 1998.

Like many of the best hookers, he played like an auxiliary flanker. A real poacher at the breakdown, he was deceptively mobile all across the pitch, providing invaluable support play. Smit was very feisty and solid at the front of the scrum and seemed to revel in the physical challenges brought by the opposition hookers. Despite his affable nature off the pitch, during the game it appeared as though Smit deliberately sought out and thrived upon direct confrontations, stepping up his game to match and even exceed the aggression of his opposite number.

As the lynchpin in the middle of the South African front row, Smit went on to play a South African record 46 consecutive test matches between 2003 and 2007, before unfortunately missing the Tri-Nations encounter with New Zealand through injury. South Africa finished last in the tournament, which was a less than ideal preparation for the impending World Cup.

But pre-tournament form went out of the window and redemption followed as Smit led the team in all seven matches, culminating in victory over reigning champions England in the final. The South African squad that year boasted several superstars in Bryan Habana, Schalk Burger and future captain Jean de Villiers, all held together by Smit.

Even after his move to France to play his club rugby with ASM Clermont Auvergne was confirmed after the World Cup, the South African Rugby Union made the unprecedented decision that Smit would retain the Springboks captaincy, despite playing his club rugby overseas.

It was a decision that paid off, as South Africa rode the wave of success after being crowned world champions. In the autumn of 2008, Smith led the Springboks to an undefeated tour of the United Kingdom, recording victories over Wales, Scotland and, most memorably, England. Their 42-6 demolition of their World Cup final opponents remains England's heaviest defeat at Twickenham and the humiliation lives long in the memory of both England and South Africa fans.

This dominance led by Smit continued still as the Springboks saw off the touring British & Irish Lions tour the next summer. Smit led by example and scored a well-worked try four minutes into the first test, which South Africa won narrowly, and despite his advancing years he played a key role in all three matches in the series.

South Africa were unstoppable and Smit completed a fantastic 2009 by winning the Tri-Nations for the first time since 2004. During this tournament he became the most-capped captain in test rugby history (a record later beaten by O'Driscoll and then further demolished by Richie McCaw).

After the Springboks exited the 2011 World Cup at the quarter-final stage, John Smit retired from international rugby, having won everything there was to win as captain of South Africa. Smit continued to play his club rugby in England for Saracens until retiring from the game completely in 2013.

42. LAWRENCE DALLAGLIO

Number eight, England 1995–2007

Lawrence Dallaglio is one of the most decorated and successful English players of all time. His career began as well as any, after emerging as a raw talent in the back row during England's victory at the 1993 Sevens World Cup. The manner in which England won seemed to set the tone for later success and you can still buy mugs featuring the image of Dallaglio's huge handoff against Australian legend Campese as he bounds away down the touchline in the final.

It's said that England struggled to get a team together for that Sevens World Cup, which allowed for the emergence of relatively unknown talent – specifically, a certain gigantic Wasps back row and a young scrum-half from Northampton named Matt Dawson. Perhaps it was a scramble for players that allowed these young players a chance to shine; with hindsight it looks something like genius.

There were many factors to England's second World Cup success: the continued partnership and understanding between Dallaglio and Dawson, the kicking ability of Wilkinson, the leadership of Johnson. But Dallaglio was the only member of the squad to play every minute of England's 2003 World Cup-winning campaign, and alongside Richard Hill and Neil Back became part of the affectionately nicknamed 'holy trinity' of back rows.

While Back and Hill provided the oft-underappreciated graft of the back row, Dallaglio dealt in aggressive and flashy ball-carrying and defence. His fire was complemented by superb skills from the base of the scrum and an expert eye for a destructive set-piece, and during the campaign he came to personify the will to win of the squad alongside captain Martin Johnson. The victory made him and Dawson the only two players, at the time, to have won both the Sevens and XV World Cups.

Dallaglio was proof that true physical strength is a real asset in the pack, the evidence that justifies all of the pack weight comparison and analysis of the impact it has on the game. His sheer size and the power with which he could drive a maul and hit a ruck were huge assets at number eight. He was an athlete through and through, with staggering and unexpected pace, which made his attacking runs somewhat reminiscent of a wrecking ball. It often took several players to bring him down once he gained momentum. But strength and speed alone are not what made Dallaglio truly great; he also possessed an outstanding rugby mind.

Not content with simply playing a crash ball when his phase duty as an attacking forward was called upon, he often found lines that are usually reserved for centres and was therefore able to draw more defenders in. He sometimes dropped back when under a kick so he was able to counter-attack using the full momentum of a man his size travelling at top speed. Few England players have scored as many important tries as this man at the back of the scrum, who always took the opportune moment to pick and go, and take the ball over the line.

What will be most memorable to English fans is his explosive and irrepressible passion. He was often on the verge of tears during a national anthem before a match and it seemed as though he played with an open wound.

That's not to say that Dallaglio's career was perfect. His was a career of ups and downs. That stunning arrival on the scene in 1993 was almost a false start and he was left out of

the 1995 World Cup. But then the dawn of the professional era had an unexpected advantage for Dallaglio as Newcastle were the first big spenders of the new Premiership and Wasps captain Rob Andrew led a mass exodus from the club to go up north. Dallaglio was then handed the captaincy of the club he loved and it was an opportunity he grabbed with both hands. His success with Wasps led to a return to the England squad, and the success spread quickly as in 1997 Dallaglio made his first appearance in a Lions shirt during the tour to South Africa, playing in all three tests of the successful series.

Dallaglio was granted the England captaincy by Clive Woodward in the autumn of 1997 following the retirement of Will Carling, but resigned his captaincy amid a storm of bad publicity in 1999 following allegations of drug dealing by the *News of the World* newspaper. Dallaglio was cleared of the most serious allegation but still fined by the RFU for 'bringing the game into disrepute'. Despite all charges being dropped, the allegations were hugely damaging to Dallaglio's status. He would later go on to emerge from this scandal free from the shackles of captaincy and repair his reputation. It's fair to say that England had not lost a leader and the selection of Martin Johnson as captain was not a bad one.

Dallaglio did indeed have a second stint in charge of England in 2004 following the retirement of Martin Johnson, but the team fared poorly in the wake of their glories of the previous year and, following a string of injuries, Dallaglio announced his own retirement from international rugby less than a year later.

However, following his recovery from injury and a Lions call-up in 2005, Dallaglio made himself available for England selection again at the end of that year. Despite Dallaglio having kept the captain Martin Corry out of the England side for the early part of his career, Corry's ability to play almost anywhere in the pack meant that there was room for Dallaglio to feature in four matches of England's 2006 Six Nations campaign, and he scored a try against Wales at Twickenham.

Despite being in the twilight of his career, Dallaglio was selected for the England squad for the 2007 World Cup, fourteen years after making that first Sevens World Cup appearance. Used as a late replacement in his second World Cup final, this was to be Dallaglio's final action in an England shirt, and a closely fought defeat to South Africa was to be his last taste of international rugby.

He secured a fairy-tale send-off when, in his final match at club level, this one-club man led Wasps to a Guinness Premiership final victory over Leicester (opposite old rival and England teammate Martin Corry) at Twickenham, receiving a standing ovation from the 81,000-strong crowd, with both sets of fans off their seats.

Many see Dallaglio as the embodiment of the courageous England forward, and his lack of success as captain should not detract from the rest of his career. He was immensely successful at the highest level and was the aggressive catalyst in what many see as the best pack in English rugby history.

41. GAVIN HASTINGS

Full-back, Scotland 1986–95

Much like the pioneering Ken Scotland in the 1950s and '60s (seen by many as the first truly attacking full-back),

Gavin Hastings scored the majority of Scotland's points as a formidable goal-kicker, leading from the back in a dynamic and brave attacking fashion and in doing so brought Scotland their best period of success in recent history.

Along with his brother Scott, Gavin Hastings made his debut in a win against an unpredictable France in the opening game of the 1986 Five Nations Championship. Scott may have had the more impressive start – a lapse in Gavin's concentration led to a French try – but crucially Gavin was dependable with the boot and kicked Scotland to an 18-17 victory. This was to be no fluke and many more assured performances followed in that year's competition, including an incredible 33-6 victory over bitter rivals England, Hastings' boot taking a vital 21 of those points in a victory that lives on in the memory of many Scottish fans.

'Big Gav' experienced further success with the British & Irish Lions as he played in all three tests in the series whitewash against Australia in 1989. His commanding performance, once more leading from the back, was insightful and defensively sound, showing his stability against world-class opposition.

The 1990 Five Nations Championship was arguably Hastings' finest moment. Momentum for the Scots was building after hard-fought victories against the Welsh and Irish, and a complete destruction of France on the way to a Murrayfield final in the closing game, against an England who were also looking for a grand slam. Although Hastings was not on kicking duty, with Craig Chalmers' goal-kicking record that year proving impressive, Big Gav's solid leadership, sturdy defence and galloping counter-attacks had charged Scotland through the competition. In the crucial decider, they relied on Hastings' wonderful handling skills and wonderful vision to chip the ball on for Tony Stanger to score in the corner and for Scotland to win what was to be their last grand slam for at least 25 years.

Cruelly though, Gavin Hastings is perhaps better remembered for one missed kick than for any of his grand slam heroics. In the dying moments of the 1991 World Cup semi-final against England, the points were level and Scotland were awarded a penalty right in front of the posts. Only 22 yards out, Hastings looked certain to score, but he was dazed following a hefty tackle from England's Micky Skinner. Hastings choked and sent the ball wide. England promptly went up the other end and Rob Andrew scored a drop-goal, denying Scotland in their best chance so far of reaching a World Cup final. Only a year before that, in a test against New Zealand, Hastings had scored a penalty from inside his own half at a tight angle. But that semi-final miss was one of the most unfortunate moments in the career of a true great.

Although Hastings played like a man possessed in the third-place play-off against New Zealand, desperate for redemption in the form of being the first Scottish side to defeat the All Blacks, it was not to be, even if in the process Hastings managed to run over the All Blacks prop Richard Loe like he wasn't there, somewhat predicting Lomu's impact four years later.

Hastings was in fact to taste victory against the All Blacks, although not for Scotland. He was selected as captain to lead the British & Irish Lions on a tour of New Zealand. He displayed commitment and great leadership and managed a test victory and was only moments from an historic series victory, which would have been only the second ever achieved by the Lions. Hastings once again showed he was marginally short of perfection. Impressive displays with the boot made him the then record test points scorer for the Lions (only now surpassed by Jonny Wilkinson).

A defining moment that lingers in the eyes of fans, showing his commitment to the Scottish cause, was a tearful interview following yet another heartbreaking defeat to England (15-14) in the Calcutta Cup clash in 1994. The heart and passion was clear for everyone to see on the pitch, and it spilled out into the post-match interview.

There were to be happier times before Hastings' retirement. In 1995, Hastings led Scotland to their first victory in 26 years on French soil. Hastings scored 18 of the 23 points that it took to beat the French team (who managed 21 points) and it was Hastings' try which made the difference. Holding on, defending for the majority of the game, Hastings displayed the hallmark of the modern fullback, shifting from solid defensive duty to galloping attacker at the perfect moment and securing the victory.

Hastings ended his international career in style at the 1995 World Cup; faced with the revelatory Jonah Lomu, Scotland adopted a bold attacking style, which ultimately failed but didn't fail to entertain as they managed to score 30 points against the All Blacks, conceding 48 in the process in one almighty entertaining send-off for the man who, on his day, was Scotland's greatest ever player.

Hastings was something of a rarity among northern hemisphere players in that he played in New Zealand, for a short time at least, and was a very respected full-back there. In 1987, although not making any test appearances, he played alongside the likes of Grant Fox, Sean Fitzpatrick and David Kirk for the University of Auckland. This experience, rubbing shoulders with some greats from the All Blacks, did no harm.

Scotland has a proud rugby tradition, but the national side has only won one Five/Six Nations Championship in the twenty years since Hastings retired. There is no doubt that his legacy and shadow hangs over Scottish rugby. But as the most impressive northern hemisphere side at the 2015 World Cup, controversially eliminated in the quarter-finals, perhaps we are at the dawn of a new era for Scotland.

40. PAUL O'CONNELL

Lock, Ireland 2001–15

Throughout the highs of back-to-back Six Nations victories and being ranked second best in the world to the lows of a group-stage elimination from a World Cup, Paul O'Connell was a talismanic mainstay for the Emerald Isle for an incredible fourteen years.

A fearless warrior and inexhaustible thief at the lineout, O'Connell was a formidable ball-carrier and a rock in the well-marshalled Irish defence. An inspired captain of his country, O'Connell was one of the greatest players Ireland has ever produced.

O'Connell made a statement of intent in his test debut against Wales in 2002, with an indication of the level to which he was prepared to push himself physically for the big occasion. Within twenty minutes he had scored a try, and after 30 minutes he had to leave the field with concussion.

Throughout the early years of his burgeoning career, he found himself under the tutorship of both Brian O'Driscoll and Keith Wood. He learned something from each of them; from Keith Wood he learned how to be an inspirational leader and have your players look up to you. From O'Driscoll he learned that a true leader should lead by example,

something O'Connell took to heart. And although he was not captain by the time he toured with the British & Irish Lions to New Zealand in 2005, comparisons were already being made to Martin Johnson, another great leader from the second row.

Ireland found great success against the home nations in these years, winning the triple crown in both 2006 and 2007, only losing out on the championships to a dominant France. Despite their finishing as runners-up in the tournament in 2007, the thrashing 43-13 of England is very fondly remembered.

Greater success would follow in 2009 when he played a key role in Ireland's historic Six Nations grand slam triumph, their first for 61 years. With O'Driscoll making the headlines in midfield, O'Connell was the colossus in the magnificent Irish pack.

His performances did not escape the attention of the Lions' selectors and he was rewarded with the captaincy of the 2009 British & Irish Lions tour to South Africa. Once again the comparisons with Martin Johnson seemed to ring true, with both players selected as tour captain while not being their national captain. O'Connell led the Lions in all three hard-fought tests in South Africa, a series that the Lions eventually lost 2-1.

After this Lions tour, O'Connell was hit by injury and was not able to compete at his best in the 2011 World Cup, nor subsequent Six Nations Championships. It is testament to his stubborn nature and physical ability that he recovered and impressed coach Warren Gatland enough to warrant a third Lions tour, this time to Australia, something very few players can boast. O'Connell's return from injury solidified him as the nation's captain and led Ireland to subsequent back-to-back Six Nations Championships in 2014 and 2015.

The Irish team under O'Connell were not as open as in previous generations. Compared to the New Zealand and Australian teams of the same era they seemed to be woefully two-dimensional in attack. But they were solid, sturdy and efficient in the breakdown. O'Connell and his pack were so competitive and physical that any team who did try to make half a break were likely to find themselves exposed and Ireland were adept at winning the ball. This Ireland team could absorb immense pressure, with some great technical place-kicking from a talented fly-half in Johnny Sexton; they would remain patient and drive forward, grind teams down and often slog out a result. The speed of play and frequency of offloading may have reduced since the departure of O'Driscoll, Ireland preferring the safe ball. Despite an absence of crowd-pleasing scattering runs in loose play, Ireland managed to find a winning formula through their discipline and strength. In more recent times, a lack of physicality in their midfield meant that Ireland were reliant on O'Connell and his back row to stretch defences and keep the ball tight.

This reliance and tight play was exposed somewhat by Argentina in the 2015 World Cup. After a heroic final group match where O'Connell and his pack fought bravely against France to avoid facing the All Blacks in the quarter-final, both Johnny Sexton and, more crucially, Paul O'Connell were ruled out of the Argentina clash. That France game was to be the last time O'Connell was to wear the green of Ireland – he was taken off on a stretcher with a torn hamstring and would be forced to watch from the sidelines as his side were torn apart by Argentina's expansive style of play. Although Ireland were the bookies' favourites, this was to prove unfounded. Los Pumas were already comfortable with the style of play needed to dismantle the Irish game

plan, which proved to be impotent without their tactician Sexton and their totemic talisman Paul O'Connell.

Ireland during the latter part of the O'Connell era didn't quite have the squad that they had enjoyed in previous years, but their hard-nosed tactics still brought them much success and caused many upsets against southern hemisphere sides who ostensibly boasted superior squads and many more 'superstars', making Ireland one of the most successful northern hemisphere teams of recent times.

39. JEREMY GUSCOTT

Centre, England 1989–99

A wonderfully cultured outside centre, Jeremy Guscott made a name for himself as the creative force behind much of the success for England and the British & Irish Lions in the 1990s.

Famously hailed as the 'Prince of Centres' by Sir Clive Woodward for his magnificent and seemingly effortless style, Guscott was legendary among fans who adored his elegant and languid running with the ability to unlock the tightest of defences. He was at his most effective when he had free rein in midfield. He was deceptively quick and always seemed aware of a gap or an unlikely cutting line, exposing the slightest slip in positioning. His awareness extended to finding the support runner, his own lines creating overlaps, and he excelled at all of the things that allow a back line to rack up points. In short, he was everything that a positive side looks for in a number thirteen.

Although it may have only been against minnows Romania, Guscott managed a hat-trick in his first international test, his immense creativity perhaps underrated as a result of the lack of fight in his opposition. It was a large jump in pressure, then, when he was immediately called up for the British & Irish Lions tour of Australia. In only his second international test – the second of the tour – Guscott managed a try and announced his arrival on to the world rugby stage as a creative force and target man, ensuring he retained his starting position for the third test. The Lions had lost the first test, and the arrival of the unknown Guscott in the two winning tests that followed was hailed as a genius piece of selection. It remains the only series in which the Lions have emerged victorious after losing the first test.

The stellar start to his career continued into the 1990 Five Nations Championship. By now he was averaging a try a game, even scoring against Scotland, who were ultimately victorious and who denied Guscott his first championship win. He did not have long to wait, however, as Guscott played a crucial role in the side that won the grand slam in both 1991 and 1992, becoming the first England side to win consecutive grand slams since 1923–24. Throughout both campaigns, Guscott provided that extra little bit of magic and quality that would unlock a stubborn defence. When facing a player of this quality, a side had to go on the offensive themselves. Guscott would force a team to play out of their comfort zone as he was always finding gaps in defence, forcing a more attacking style of play in retaliation, undoing whatever game plan they set out with. When playing outside a solid player like Simon Halliday, who did much of the defensive work for Jeremy, England were able to afford the luxury of a roaming Guscott. Not only was this effective for England, but it was wonderful for spectators.

Guscott continued as the bright spark for England and on the almost-successful '93 Lions tour, until injury ruined his 1994 season. He recovered in time for another Five Nations grand slam in 1995, forming a formidable partnership with Will Carling. Following this success he went on to participate in England's humiliation at the hands of Jonah Lomu and New Zealand in the 1995 World Cup. After Carling and Mike Catt were bulldozed, Guscott's apparent lack of defensive capabilities was perhaps a problem against an opponent such as the All Blacks. On the harder pitches of South Africa, Guscott should have been allowed to shine, but England were unable to establish a foothold against New Zealand and their tactics did not play to the strengths of their outside centre.

The centre combination of Will Carling and Jeremy Guscott remained a fruitful one, but with Phil de Glanville made captain – for his leadership qualities more than his playing abilities – Carling was moved to outside centre and there was no room for Guscott in the starting line-up. In the 1996 Five Nations, Guscott remarkably found himself on the bench, making appearances as a replacement to great effect. A real crowd-pleaser, it was decided that Guscott was a luxury they could afford, despite the increasing physicality required to play in midfield.

Jeremy Guscott made his third and final Lions tour in 1997, this time to South Africa. He started each test playing outside the very physical ex-league player Scott Gibbs, who much like Simon Halliday allowed Guscott all kinds of freedom. One of Guscott's most glorious moments came in that second test victory over the Springboks, a rare, sweetly struck drop-goal which once again proved that if nothing else you could trust Jeremy Guscott to be wonderfully unpredictable. Guscott broke his arm twenty minutes into the third test, which the

Lions would lose (with the tour already won) and injury once again put a halt to the 32-year-old's career.

Although reduced to a bit part by this stage, Guscott made his final England appearance in the 101-10 devastation of Tonga during the 1999 World Cup. He scored two tries and received a standing ovation from the crowd. He was subsequently dropped for the play-off against Fiji and didn't feature in the quarter-final loss against South Africa. Guscott continued to play for Bath until the end of that season before retiring aged 35. Jeremy Guscott will be best remembered by English fans for his gift of effortless grace under pressure, as well as for making the most trying aspects of the game look easy – the mark of real talent.

38. KEITH WOOD

Hooker, Ireland 1994–2003

Together with Syd Millar, another Irish rugby great, Gordon Wood was one of the stars of the 1959 British & Irish Lions tour to Australia. The tighthead prop went on to make a further 29 appearances for Ireland, scoring one try. So it was fitting that it was against Australia that his son Keith made his own debut, bursting on to the scene as one of the most promising forwards Ireland has ever seen.

Keith Wood went on to become one of Ireland's most iconic rugby players. An incredibly driven player, Wood excelled at hooker both for Ireland and the British & Irish Lions in a career that equalled and then surpassed his father's.

Right from the start of his career he was known for his

head-down, charging attacking runs, with startling mobility for a hooker of his stature. Although he was always keen to show versatility (the defensive side-step that threw two Australians and allowed him to clear the danger with a long kick in the 1999 World Cup springs to mind), it was the damaging head-on runs that made the impact and led to a try-scoring record for a hooker – his tally of fifteen test tries from that position is still unequalled.

Wood rewrote the book for what was expected from hookers. He was not content with simply throwing the ball into the lineout and scrummaging. You don't find many hookers who can handle the highly technical aspects of the position and still find room for the athleticism and all of the 'extra' that Wood brought with him. He covered more of the park than most and was often found among the back three, kicking back – and often finding touch better than established kickers. Much of this astounding versatility was down to his mental ability under pressure and his desire to lead by example. Along with the aforementioned cheeky side-stepping, the charging runs, the astounding kicks and the crucial tries, Wood had superb handling skills and was always found tracking back to make try-saving tackles. That isn't to say he neglected his more combative duties, although his positioning may have seemed more like that of a full-back than of a tight forward.

Despite showing huge promise during his international debut against Australia in Brisbane in 1994, Wood only managed one appearance at his first Rugby World Cup in 1995, as he was in the unfortunate position of being in the shadow of captain Terry Kingston. This was a selector's headache, as there was only room for one player – and the promise shown by the young forward wasn't enough to displace the captain just yet.

But the potential was there, and after Kingston's retirement in 1996, Wood was an automatic selection. Wood played in an Ireland side that never won the Six Nations and only defeated England once in the tournament (in 2001; Wood scored a try that day), and still it seemed as though his best performances were against the top teams. In November 1997, he scored his first two international tries against the All Blacks, no less, something few can claim (and something no other hooker has ever achieved). The second try in particular embodied the spirit of Wood's Ireland. Seemingly incensed by New Zealand's arrogant flat attacking line, Wood led a defensive line which pounced upon and trapped a particularly complacent move, turning the ball over in the process. Ireland pushed on the counter and quickly made ground, with Wood chasing the kick over the top and producing a finish that any winger would be proud of.

This was off the back of a spectacular showing on the Lions' victorious tour of South Africa in 1997. Wood was one of the most charismatic leaders in the game at the time, and indeed it could have been tough for the squad to incorporate both Wood and tour captain Martin Johnson, but Wood backed up his captain with some inspirational displays and truly proved himself as one of the world's best players.

Wood experienced his share of disappointment and frustration representing Ireland, but played his part in his second Rugby World Cup in 1999 as they lost out to Argentina in a quarter-final play-off. Following that, Wood toured with the Lions again, playing all three tests against Australia in 2001. They were less successful on this occasion, losing the series 2-1. The end result notwithstanding, Wood was in the form of his life and capped off an outstanding year by being named the inaugural World Rugby Player of the Year. He remains the only Irishman and the only hooker to be given the award, once again proving that Wood was undoubtedly a talented player but perhaps not playing at the right time to be surrounded by teammates capable of winning trophies.

This personal success was followed a swift downfall; his 2002 season was blighted by injury and he only played in one Six Nations game, aggravating a neck injury in the process. Wood would struggle to return from injury to captain his country in the 2003 Rugby World Cup, his third, immediately retiring after their 43-21 quarter-final loss to France. That isn't to say his career ended with a whimper – during that 2003 World Cup campaign, Wood produced some of the best rugby of his career. But the heartache and physical endurance seemed too much for him; he ended the match in tears, but had cemented his place as a true hero of Irish rugby.

37. TIM HORAN

Centre, Australia 1989–2000

A man who was regarded as one of the best midfielders in the world, Australia's Tim Horan played a huge part in establishing the Wallabies' dominance throughout the 1990s.

In an international career spanning eleven years, Tim Horan joined that rare and elite group of players to have won two World Cups. In that time Horan notched up 80 caps and scored 30 tries for his country and will be best remembered for tearing defences apart as a playmaker inside the legendary David Campese.

Horan played in an Australian back line that had skill in abundance. He came to prominence just as the foundations laid by the likes of Mark Ella and Campese were being fully realised. The World Cup in 1991 saw the Wallabies become the second nation to win the coveted trophy. Australia had a difficult route to the final and faced a tougher test against the All Blacks in the semi-final than they did against England in the final. It took all the skill of Horan, Michael Lynagh and David Campese to defeat their New Zealand rivals. This impressive back line had an almost telepathic relationship and their synchronisation was on show as they scored a magnificent team try, one of the greatest the World Cup has ever seen, for importance as well as skill. After several phases of well-worked tight play, the ball was spread wide and Campese broke the line and after side-stepping full-back Kieran Crowley, found himself being caught by the All Blacks defence. A blind pass found Horan, who was exactly where Campese had hoped he'd be, and he raced to the try line. Although often overshadowed by the brilliance of Campese, Horan scored four tries in the tournament and was instrumental to Australia's success.

Throughout his career, he was able to adapt his game and grow as a player. In the Australian midfield, he formed memorable partnerships with Jason Little and latterly Daniel Herbert. Little was a more traditional outside centre; with great handling and vision, he worked well with Horan. But as the modern breed of centre arrived on the scene in the form of straight-running powerhouse Herbert, Horan was able to adapt his game to carve a reputation as one of the most well-balanced centres the game has ever seen.

The Australia team of the '90s was not only highly successful, but played some of the most technically breathtaking rugby in the history of the sport. Many saw the team as a real breath of fresh air against the perceived negative forward-based play of England and goal-kicking tactics of the All Blacks.

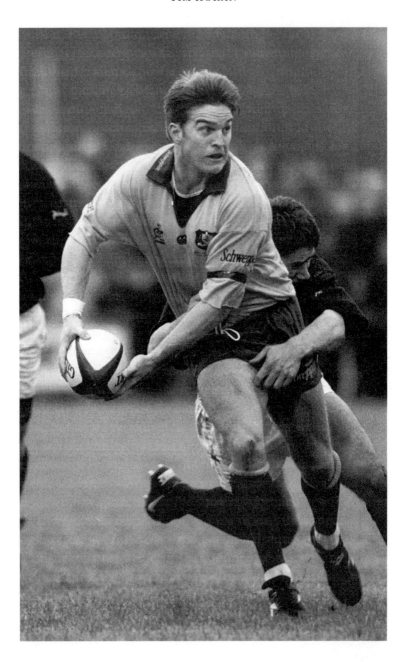

Horan made strong use of his talents and was as astute defensively as he was on the attack. Combining physical prowess, tactical understanding and alertness with a great rugby mind meant that Horan seemed tailor-made for the midfield and had no weak points to his game whatsoever. This intelligence and awareness on the pitch saw Horan improve continuously, playing arguably some of his best rugby in the twilight stages of his career.

But it was not just invention and intelligence that led to his growth as a player; it was necessity. Suffering horrific knee ligament damage while playing for Queensland in 1994, his battle to return was incredibly tough and the injury nearly ended his career entirely. After extensive rehabilitation, he returned to the Wallabies side just in time for his second World Cup in 1995, but was not back to his best yet. Australia suffered a narrow defeat to England in the quarter-final, but it was just the start of Horan's return.

It was at the 1999 World Cup that Horan arguably eclipsed his 1991 exploits, scoring two tries – his first coming only 92 seconds into the tournament, against Romania. His standout performance came against the Springboks in the semi-final. Despite reportedly suffering from food poisoning the night before, Horan battled through the game. A controlling force for the Wallabies in their hard-fought extra-time victory, Horan then performed well in seeing off France in the final to be named player of the tournament. Even when compared to the mighty Jonah Lomu who amassed eight tries in that tournament, there was little argument with the accreditation.

So important was Horan to his side that he never started a single game from the bench. Every time he was fit, he was the first name on the team sheet. An iconic Wallabies player and great ambassador for the sport, Tim Horan retired from international rugby a year after winning his second World Cup medal and continued his club rugby in England for Saracens until retiring from the game completely in 2003.

36. MERVYN DAVIES

Number eight, Wales 1969–76

Merv 'the Swerve' Davies was the greatest forward to ever don the Welsh jersey. He was as instrumental to the success of Gareth Edwards and the Wales side of the 1970s as any other player, arguably even more so than Barry John or Phil Bennett at fly-half. His absolute command at the back of the lineout also set a new benchmark for all future number eights.

Mervyn Davies left behind a legacy that few other Welsh players have ever matched, and was loved by his teammates to the same extent that he was feared by his opposition. Although he was fortunate to have played for Wales when he did and featured in the real golden era for the Lions, the record stands that Davies lost just 9 of the 46 games that he played in for Wales and the British Lions.

And it's not just the match-win record: Davies also won the trophies to accompany it. He led Wales to two grand slams and three triple crowns and his national team's decade of dominance of the rugby world.

Wales were in a transitional period in 1969: number eight Davies made his international debut alongside the fresh-faced Barry John and superlative Gareth Edwards, and

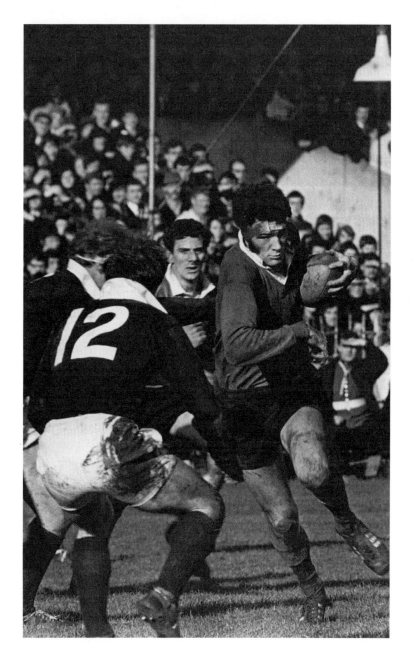

although he would not officially become captain until 1975, every great team needs a leader and in the intervening years his influence in overseeing and bringing together the pool of talent was colossal.

Although Wales were yet at their best, making a stuttering start in 1969, Davies won a triple crown in his first full international season before the incredible grand slam year of 1971.

This led to his selection for the Lions' famous tour of New Zealand in 1971. In fact, Merv's part in the Welsh success that year meant that, appropriately, far more Welshmen were selected for this tour than representatives of any of the other home nations. After having suffered a heavy tour defeat three years before, the Lions won the series with Davies starting all four tests in the back row alongside the likes of Peter Dixon and the future commentator John Taylor.

This success set a precedent and Davies was an indelible presence as Welsh rugby grew from strength to strength. But despite their illustrious history in this sport, Wales are not historically known for their heroic forwards, and indeed in this golden era the backs reigned supreme and stole the headlines. Wales's sheer dominance of teams could not come simply from the flashy back line – the possession was won by the perhaps less headline-worthy hard-working pack – but Davies' rangy presence alongside his fellow forwards was somewhat overshadowed nonetheless.

In 1974, Davies was included in his second Lions squad, this time to tour South Africa, in one of the most violent tours that international rugby has ever seen. Davies again played all four test matches and helped the Lions complete a more infamous than famous unbeaten tour. This was a physical tour, with on-pitch fighting and mass brawls. Davies was not a thug – or indeed that large for a number eight –

but neither did he shy away from a confrontation. Although the violence was certainly not one-sided, what the Lions managed that the South Africans couldn't was play rugby throughout the carnage.

Among Davies' many great contributions was to make sure he was always first to the breakdown. Although not the fastest man on the pitch, his ability to read the game, and anticipate the movements of play, meant that Davies never left the ball-carrier stranded.

Throughout his career, Davies was able to combine the simple basics with a staggeringly consistent grace. An incredibly technical tackler, he made every textbook movement a matter of routine. And such a reliable force in the pack allowed for the orchestration of a collection of choreographed moves from the back line, causing havoc with opposition midfields.

Davies' leadership skills were recognised formally late in his career – he was only handed the captaincy of Wales in 1975 – but his record as captain was flawless, guiding his side to the Five Nations Championship that year and the grand slam the following season.

And just as it seemed as though his career was reaching its peak and he was being widely touted as the man to lead the 1977 Lions, Davies had his career cut short by horrific injury. Merv 'the Swerve' Davies was playing for Swansea during a Welsh Cup semi-final clash with Pontypool in 1976 when he suffered an intracranial brain haemorrhage and was forced to retire from the game at the age of 29.

35. BILL BEAUMONT

Lock, England 1975–84

Bill Beaumont led English rugby through one of its least successful periods ever, ending the team's 23-year wait for a Five Nations grand slam in the process. Although he may be better remembered as a long-serving captain on the BBC's *A Question of Sport*, before those television-friendly years, Beaumont was a hard-nosed England captain.

Beaumont made his debut in 1977, at a time when the odds were stacked against England, and was on the losing side seven times in his first eight test matches. Throughout this time, Beaumont stood out as an accomplished lock forward who never did anything fancy, never made a cheeky drop-goal or many marauding runs through the midfield, but he did his job and he did it well. What England were crying out for at the time was some stability, an inspiring leader and a platform for success.

Beaumont first truly made a name for himself as a last-minute replacement following injuries to both Nigel Horton and Geoff Wheel on the 1977 British & Irish Lions tour of New Zealand. Dealing with the added pressure of not being first or even second choice for the starting role, he impressed as a replacement in the final warm-up game of the tour and earned himself a place in the test side. Surrounded by more successful – and better – players than with England, he could really show his worth. Beaumont took over as England captain the next year, also making appearances for the Barbarians against a touring All Blacks side.

1979 proved to be the start of something special for

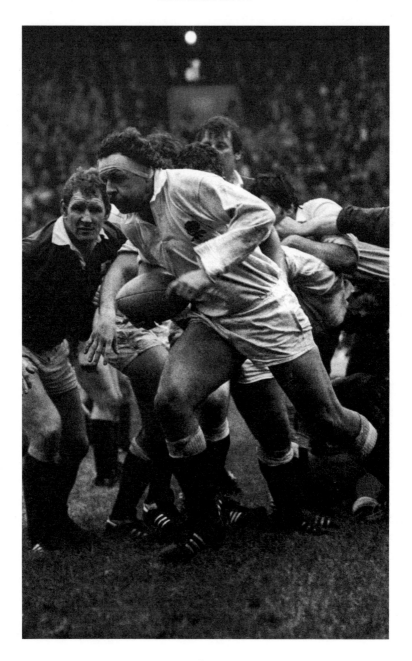

Beaumont as he captained a provincial North of England side in a warm-up game for yet another touring All Blacks side (the previous year's tourists having returned to New Zealand unbeaten). Facing players such as Stu Wilson, Graham Mourie and Andy Haden, nobody gave the North of England much of a chance, but they whipped the All Blacks 21-9. That North of England side contained players such as a young Fran Cotton and Roger Uttley, but at the time they were hardly world-beaters. Uttley, in fact, was only at the start of his career. It was games like this that gave England, led by Beaumont, hope for the future.

The hope was not misplaced, as 1980 was Beaumont's finest year. He captained England to their first Five Nations grand slam since 1957, defeating both Wales and France, who had dominated the competition for over a decade. While it's true that many of the French and Welsh stars were past their best and retiring, this was no mean feat and Beaumont was rewarded with the captaincy of the next British & Irish Lions tour. Travelling to South Africa as the first English captain of the Lions for 50 years was a great honour. They only managed one test victory on this tour against the Springboks, but the Lions pack dominated throughout and Beaumont's leadership was exemplary. They were let down by a weak back line, untried and untested following the retirement of many of the heroes from the '70s, and they were shown up by the vastly experienced South African side.

What made him so great is that Beaumont would charge around the pitch hitting the rucks at full speed, clearing them out with perfect timing. This was no aimless act, he would not simply follow the ball, but was an excellent tactician and inspirational leader.

Beaumont retired in 1982 aged 34 and it was to be another nine years before England were to enjoy success again.

The next time England enjoyed success there was a whole generation of greats. Will Carling, Rory Underwood and Jeremy Guscott were to be the future of English rugby – in the meantime England had Beaumont.

34. JASON ROBINSON

Full-back, England 2001–07

Rugby history is littered with code switchers, some more successful than others. For a long time the trend was to go from rugby union to the more lucrative league; of course, that was before the professional era, which has led to a reverse trend.

Along with Wendell Sailor, Israel Folau and Sonny Bill Williams, Jason Robinson was one of the few players of the modern era who thrived in both codes. There are some that have a short career before making the switch and others who seem to spend their twilight years with the other code. But there are few who played both with quite the impact of Robinson – and it has to be remembered that he has made this list purely for his exploits in rugby union. Robinson was 26 when he made the switch; during his rugby league career he had excelled for Wigan as they reigned supreme over the Super League, and represented both Great Britain and England.

He made his England debut against Italy in the 2001 Six Nations, only three months after making the switch, and was subsequently selected for the British & Irish Lions tour to Australia that summer. He scored a staggering five tries on

his Lions debut in a less than challenging warm-up match against Western Australia. This performance was enough to earn a place in the starting line-up for the first test against the Wallabies, in which he scored a stunning solo try. Robinson made the difficult transition from league to union look easy and already looked like a world-class player.

Often referred to as Billy Whizz, which was one of the more literal and obvious in the great history of rugby union nicknames, Robinson had an outrageous side-step as well as a bucketload of raw acceleration. What made Billy special was that he was a player who did not particularly rely on his teammates for success. There are few players in the history of the game who were able to galvanise their team with such an individual display.

Although incredibly destructive on the wing, where he played many games, including for the British & Irish Lions and indeed for England in the 2003 World Cup final, full-back is where he was best. Reliable under a high ball, he was able to tear through a staggered opposition time and time again in counter-attack. The change of pace was so extraordinary that it seemed like someone pressed the fast-forward button when he received the ball. Playing at full-back gave him the opportunity to watch the defensive line and spot gaps, and when one appeared, he only needed a split-second to break through.

That's not to say that his game was without weak spots. Robinson's defence was good enough, if not excellent, but he never seemed comfortable kicking out of hand. That's quite a price to pay but there aren't many teams that wouldn't select their back three to accommodate one of the most dangerous attacking players rugby union has ever seen. That said, against a team such as Australia in the World Cup final, Woodward decided to play Robinson on the wing in order to make room for Josh Lewsey as a more robust defensive player at full-back. Throughout the game this back three were very fluid and of course the tactical decision paid off as Robinson scored England's only try in that famous victory.

Following the 2003 World Cup he briefly captained England while Jonny Wilkinson was out injured, but he announced his retirement from international rugby following the 2005 Lions tour to New Zealand, where he won two further test caps in what was a complete whitewash and returned home defeated.

In what was to be his final season playing club rugby in 2006/07, Robinson won the Guinness Premiership title with Sale. It was during this season that he was coaxed out of retirement by the new England coach Brian Ashton ahead of the 2007 Six Nations, to provide leadership qualities and a match-winning mentality that England had lacked following the retirement of Martin Johnson and other key forwards, along with injuries to Wilkinson and others. Accusations that he was picked purely for added experience and as a talisman were soon proven to be unfounded as he continued his brutal try-scoring record with three tries in his first two games back.

Before the tournament, Robinson announced that the World Cup would be the last games of professional rugby he would play. Throughout a run of disappointing performances for England, he remained one of the few consistent performers as they scraped through the group stages and stuttered to a final against all probability. In what was a slightly lacklustre final by World Cup standards, Robinson was forced off injured, leaving England to lose 15-6 amid speculation on how the result would have gone had the veteran full-back not left the field early in the second half.

Robinson's time playing rugby league was plagued with

well-documented off-the-field problems, but he overcame many, including alcoholism, to become a world champion. He was one of the few players of England's golden era to be a fans' favourite outside of England, a real bright spark in a team infamous for a perceived reliance on the boot of Wilkinson. One thing is for sure: the crowd stood when Robinson received the ball. Right through to the end of his career, Billy Whizz was a player who for a spectator would make the hairs on the back of the neck stand on end in anticipation, and who will be remembered as one of the sport's great entertainers.

33. SERGIO PARISSE

Number eight, Italy 2002–

Sergio Parisse is a warrior with magnificent technical ability and awareness, combined with resolute leadership skills; he is the greatest rugby player his country has ever produced. He raised the profile of the sport in his native Italy, not just with his on-the-pitch exploits, but with lucrative sponsorship and high-profile modelling assignments, in the process becoming one of the most recognisable stars of European rugby and the face of the Azzurri.

Regardless of his status as the poster boy of Italian rugby, all things considered, he is simply one of the best number eights ever to have played the game. Comfortably taking his place alongside the likes of Zinzan Brooke, Lawrence Dallaglio and Mervyn Davies, Parisse brings another dimension and has had to contend with something that the others have not: those guys all played in dominant sides, shoulder to shoulder with world-class players, whereas Parisse has made his name on the back foot, losing the majority of his games for his country, while experiencing many great victories at club level with Stade Français.

Parisse possesses many of the skills more commonly found in southern hemisphere forwards. His handling ability, vision and superb timing on the ball are things that are all too rarely found in a number eight in the Six Nations Championship. He is able to give his side another great option at the foot of the scrum. Reaching the breakdown and as capable as the next back row at clearing and securing the ball, he's also able to play the ball under intense pressure. His range of passing is impressive, his distribution capable of throwing the opposition off the scent and starting the most penetrating of Italian attacking moves. A consistent performer, Parisse is always at the centre of every great performance from his team. His handling and technical abilities do not come at a cost: he is still a powerful ball-carrier, able to smash through the gain line with brute strength and athleticism. His commitment and bravery make him an extra lineout option and he will almost never be caught out of position or missing tackles.

Italy joined the annual competition that would henceforth be called the Six Nations Championship in the year 2000. Their entrance was met with scepticism from many who believed they would simply prove to be whipping boys, favourites for the wooden spoon, year in, year out. Their first three years, unsurprisingly, did little to prove these critics wrong, with not a single victory.

Parisse made his debut for Italy aged just eighteen in 2002, in a 64-10 away defeat to New Zealand. It was not simply a baptism of fire for the young forward; this one-sided display

was to serve as useful preparation for the future captain, who would have to endure many miserable days and uphill battles to keep Italy competitive over the years. Parisse was to prove he had the mental strength and controlled competitive nature required to be a leader of the perennial underdogs, and still display the individual quality and consistency required to improve.

Parisse was not yet a first-team regular by the time Italy recorded their first ever Six Nations victory over Wales in 2003. Then a junior member of the squad, Parisse has been involved in Italy's battle for recognition, and part of the generation who have worked hard on raising the Azzurri's reputation in the 21st century. Ever since his first game, Parisse has been aware that he was going to have to shoulder the disappointment inevitably felt by a competitive athlete in defeat, and must remain inspirational enough to fight back and retain confidence.

Italy improved steadily with Parisse as captain. Despite the final result not always favouring the Azzurri, their performances and standard of play saw a vast improvement. In 2007 Italy managed two wins in the Six Nations Championship for the first time, finishing fourth in the competition. Importantly, their comfortable victory over Scotland came at Murrayfield, banishing the horrific record that Italy had had away from home, lifting a mental barrier and bringing a new-found confidence to the side. Their other victory in that tournament was a magical tie against Wales, where Italy came from behind to record a 23-20 win. Parisse was man of the match that day, and the man who made the difference and held his nerve. A test that close requires mental strength and leadership. Despite crashing out of the pool stages of the World Cup that year, Parisse was recognised by the IRB and was nominated for World Player of the Year, placing him alongside players of the pedigree of Shane Williams and Dan Carter.

A potentially meteoric rise was put on hold as a serious knee injury ruled him out of an entire season, but he fought his way back to inspire Italy's first win against France in the Six Nations in 2011. The most important effect of this victory was the instilled belief that, with Parisse, Italy could win again.

Throughout all of these victories, Parisse's consistent talent remained. His ball-carrying ability, his lineout presence and his canny running into open channels in broken play were always felt. But nothing was felt more keenly than his calming and inspirational presence in the squad.

There have been occasions where Italy have felt like a one-man side, the limitations of his teammates leaving Parisse somewhat of an isolated figure, standing alone and overwhelmed by his opposition. However, as Parisse progressed, so did his teammates. Martín Castrogiovanni, playing at prop, has provided much-needed relief from some of the physical work, as well as proving himself to be an excellent scrummager, whereas Andrea Masi has brought some vision and creativity to the back line at full-back. Through all of this, Parisse has remained the talisman, Italy's greatest hope and the one the spectators look to.

In 2012, they managed another Six Nations win, albeit against recent strugglers Scotland, but the margins of defeat against the other sides were no longer as wide. Indeed, they almost defeated England in Rome, but poor discipline allowed England to kick their way to victory despite two Italian tries and the match finished 15-19. Parisse's reputation continued to rise throughout this time and he was utterly key in Italy's famous win over France in the opening game of the 2013 tournament. Rome had become a real fortress for the Azzurri and they astonishingly defeated Ireland there, setting up a finale in which, for the first time in Six Nations history, Italy had a (admittedly very slim) chance of winning the championship. While they lost the last game heavily, their belief made this tournament a real watershed moment for Italy.

Parisse himself has been a superb servant for Italy who could probably have walked into any national side in the world, including the All Blacks. But it was not simply his individual talent that marked him out. Sergio Parisse has inspired the younger players, and while he is not ready to retire yet, the hole that will be left when he does leave will hopefully be filled by many young Azzurri who have benefited from the world-class presence in their squad.

Since joining the Six Nations, Italy's improvement has not been consistent; there have been a few false dawns, followed by a wooden spoon. It has certainly contrasted with Argentina's improvement since joining the Rugby Championship, which has been far steeper. Despite this, the Azzurri are in a far healthier position nowadays – a fact almost entirely down to Parisse – and the future looks bright. It's only a matter of time before they defeat England in a test – especially since they have defeated stronger Welsh and Irish sides – and truly start challenging for the title.

32. SERGE BLANCO

Full-back, France 1980–91

Even in a side renowned for their flair and excitement, Serge Blanco stood out as one of the most immediately exciting and innovative counter-attacking players the game has ever seen.

Seen as a utility back by France over the years, starting at wing and sometimes used at centre, he looked at his most brilliant and effective when at full-back. For such a rare player, full-back gave him the free rein he needed to create. Like the best innovators, his judgement was not always flawless and he was sometimes exposed at centre and sometimes ineffective on the wing. But at full-back he was at his breathless best on the counter-attack, thrilling spectators for more than a decade.

His most identifiable trait was an incredible turn of pace. From a standing start he could be at full acceleration almost immediately, and was particularly devastating should any misplaced tactical kick not find touch. His presence at the back was one that his opposition was more than aware of and it only took one devastating counter-attack to make any tactical kicking-heavy opposition rethink their whole approach.

It is somewhat jarring in light of his utter athleticism that he should also have been a heavy smoker, although looked at another way, it perhaps suggests a nonchalance that is very much in keeping with his spellbinding and charismatic play.

It was not that Blanco's game was without weakness; far from it. In his international debut against South Africa in 1980, he oversaw a porous defence which conceded five tries. It took the French side a while to adjust to Blanco as the last line of defence, as this was not his priority. Indeed, at this time Les Bleus were erratic: unbeatable at their best, but liable to collapse, with organisation and consistency taking a back seat to flair, ingenuity and creativity. During a simultaneously entertaining and frustrating era for France, Serge Blanco broke the mould for full-backs as a truly volatile and threatening counter-attacking player who longed for open play.

But his initial stint at full-back didn't last too long; Blanco was moved to the wing where he took part in the 1981 grand slam, scoring a try against Scotland and generally looking impressive without quite standing out as a star player. His brilliance wasn't truly felt until after working hard on his kicking game he moved back to full-back.

That's not to say his defence was poor, more that his physical presence was simply not like that of J.P.R. Williams or other contemporary full-backs. At his outlandish best when putting his skill and ambitious innovation to use in attack, he applied a similar approach to his defensive game, with varying degrees of success. In a one-on-one situation he would use his speed and positional savvy to force the attacker into making the wrong decision, and would sometimes back himself into an area with no support, or out into touch. This use of his tactical instinct could be implemented at the highest speed, showing the defender one way and using his turn of pace to close the gap. It did not work all of the time: when confronted Blanco did not always have the physicality to bring down the heaviest of runners. But his all-or-nothing approach fed through into all aspects of his game.

Scoring vital tries for Les Bleus over the years was not the only measure of Blanco's attacking prowess. Blanco had the audacity to do what many of his contemporaries would not: he would run it out of defence when it certainly did not look like the best option but, charging along his own line, he would create a space to allow a teammate to make a promising run down a now-clear line, turning the most dire of defensive situations into try-scoring opportunities. I'm sure coaches throughout the land were livid as young full-backs attempted to emulate this, only to leave their team in a world of trouble.

Indeed, following the rule change decades before to

prevent teams kicking straight to touch from anywhere on the pitch, the trend had moved towards the more attacking full-back as they were more than the last line of defence with a good kick. Blanco probably represented the end of the purely attacking full-back as the game developed and once again a defensive and indeed more balanced full-back became necessary. Blanco belonged to a very specific time, and is a symbol for the beauty and style of French rugby.

Although his irregularity and defensive weakness were there for all to see – he could rarely be depended on to make a last-ditch tackle – Blanco could not be accused of a lack of commitment. As is common with a naturally gifted talent, his game could appear effortless. His nonchalance and grace under pressure, coupled with his erratic form, could sometimes lead to absolute anonymity for long periods. Indeed, Blanco could go an entire 80 minutes without having much impact on the game at all. However, he was one who was able to step up to the occasion, as could be witnessed during the 1987 World Cup when he scored an injury-time try, securing France's place in the final. Blanco celebrated with ecstasy, almost overcome with emotion, destroying his cool and unflappable image forever – in the process endearing him to an entire generation.

For someone whose speed and agility were an integral part of his play, Blanco endured over a decade of international test rugby. However, his speed was starting to diminish by the time of the 1991 World Cup, although his creative spark pushed France to the top of their group and a quarter-final against hosts England. This was to prove his last game and the only time before 2015 that France did not make the World Cup semi-finals. Serge Blanco retired after scoring 38 tries in a staggering 93 test appearances, still the record for a Frenchman. He retired as a great of the game, revered throughout the world as one of the game's most entertaining and innovative sparks.

31. MARK ELLA

Fly-half, Australia 1980–84

Mark Ella was a fly-half who couldn't kick, didn't have a lot of pace, and wasn't the strongest in the tackle, but whose unique vision lives on and whose name is so revered by the Australian fans that he more than justifies his place on our list. This is made all the more surprising when you consider that he retired at the age of 25.

Ella was a star of the famous Australian Schoolboys squad that toured Britain undefeated in 1978, but truly caught the attention of spectators when he lined up alongside twin brother Glen and younger brother Gary in 1981 to become the first trio of brothers ever to be selected for the Wallabies.

It was with his brothers that he experimented with an innovative flat back line style. He would stand very close to his scrum-half, easing the pressure from the initial pass and confusing the opposition back row. This flat line relied on the half-backs' ability to work under the inevitable pressure they were putting themselves under and required perfect handling skills. By removing his thinking time, Ella put the pressure back on the defence: one false move and they would have broken through.

This exceptional skill caught the attention of the rugby elite when Ella shut Hugo Porta out of the game against Argentina in 1983. But it is his final test season, the grand slam tour of Britain and Ireland, for which Ella is best remembered. He scored tries in each of the four test matches against England, Ireland, Scotland and Wales – something a touring player had never before achieved.

The Australia team of 1984 laid the foundations for their reputation today and Mark Ella epitomised their revolutionary attitude and style. He was the poster boy for that side, just as their dominance was showing on the world stage. But after returning home as a superstar, he never played for his country again.

What is more astonishing about that tour is that every one of Mark's tries came from his own brilliance; a truly instinctive player, Ella found attacking lines to run with perfectly executed choreography. Every move seemed at once to be the result of several painstakingly refined hours on the training pitch, but improvised to perfection, and he left the defence stranded.

Although this almost telepathic style of play was developed with his brothers, it was his relationship with Aussie hero David Campese that saw his tactics most effectively utilised. Having Campese's raw power and talent outside of him proved to be a lethal partnership and Ella was described by Campese as 'the best rugby player I have ever known or seen'.

Like the best fly-halves, he was not content to sit back after making the delivery; he got involved with the attack. His off-the-ball running found him making and receiving several passes on his way to completing a try outside the winger. This trait, seen more and more in the modern game, is Ella's legacy. His try against Ireland in 1984 is a great example: after creating the overlap, he found himself both starting and ending a superb team try.

If you had to name one defining feature of Mark Ella's success, it would be his phenomenal support play. The vision

he showed in continually popping up in exactly the right place after making a pass, and in so doing creating a gap for the player outside of him to break the line, was often match-winning. Simply making himself available again in attacking play was the catalyst for much of Australia's success, including victory against New Zealand in Ella's first ever test in 1980. He managed this without ever seeming to have a sense of urgency. A three-quarter pace was his default setting, as he rarely needed to sprint.

Mark Ella was as much of an entertainer as he was a match-winner. His try against Wales in his penultimate test match serves to illustrate this point. The try was not a match-winner – it was in injury time in a test that Australia had already won. Wales were on the attack in very loose play, Mark Ella ran an interception and, quick as a shot, managed to prove he was capable not only of sprinting, but also of scoring every type of try there is for a half-back to score.

When looking back at Ella's career, there is a certain element of what might have been. You have to wonder what would have happened if he hadn't hung up his boots aged 25; what other innovations would he have brought to the game and would he be remembered as fondly without the romance of having retired so young?

His reasons for retiring seem a little mysterious still. Money does not seem to have been behind it, as it was for many others in this pre-professional era, as he never even flirted with the idea of switching codes, despite offers. There are rumours of fallings-out with coaches, of him losing the captaincy at the hands of new coach Alan Jones. Among other contradictory comments on the matter, Ella has stated that he wished he could have played in a World Cup, the inaugural event occurring three years after his retirement. He said that had he known there was to be a World Cup, and stadia as full as they were, he would have played on for sure.

Wales legend Gareth Edwards said that the Aussies lost a bit of spark behind the scrum when Ella retired – even though Michael Lynagh was a great rugby player and was certainly world-class in terms of his point-scoring ability. But it was true: Australia lost something very rare indeed when Ella retired, that they have often tried, but have never quite managed, to emulate.

30. MIKE GIBSON

Fly-half/centre, Ireland 1964–79

For those who preferred the rugby union of a bygone era, Mike Gibson will quite possibly be considered the finest Irish player ever. Even taking Brian O'Driscoll into account, Gibson must certainly rank as the most naturally gifted. A real pioneer of the back line, controlling play and bridging the gap between positions, Gibson's versatility and vision were way ahead of his time.

This versatility led to some positional question marks and although Gibson started as a fly-half, he moved to centre and even occasionally turned out on the wing. In truth, this was as much down to his own brilliance and flexibility as the desire to accommodate other players, both for Ireland and for the British & Irish Lions. His sensational handling and vision were complemented by an excellent kicking game, his tactical awareness giving him the ability to excel both at centre and outside half. His greatest moments of magic, however, were made from the midfield position.

Gibson's breezy, attractive style left a real impression on Irish rugby, laying the foundations for modern greats like Brian O'Driscoll and Gordon D'Arcy. But Gibson was a more delicate and subtle centre than many crash-ball, bulky midfield players of recent years, preferring to unlock a defence with a carefully timed deceptive dummy, a silky pass, or thorough and intrusive support play rather than bludgeoning a team into submission. His understanding of the game, his opposition and the angles needed was flawless and watching Gibson at his best was a thing of beauty.

Mike Gibson made his debut at outside half against England at Twickenham in the 1964 Five Nations Championship, making an instant impression and inspiring a comprehensive victory as the creator of two crucial tries. With expert timing, Gibson broke through the middle of the English line, the all-important breakaway which led to their opening try. A second moment of genius soon followed: Gibson left the English midfield scratching their heads with a dummy move and a sleek pass, slipping his winger through for another superb try. This proved to be Ireland's only victory of the competition, however, and they finished bottom of the table. Despite Ireland boasting some great players, like Gibson and Willie John McBride, the late 1960s and the '70s were dominated entirely by the Welsh and the French, with Ireland's only championship victory featuring Gibson coming in 1974.

In common with certain other players of this era, Gibson's legend was forged playing with the British & Irish Lions. Indeed it was with the Lions that he first played at centre, to accommodate the Welsh outside half David Watkins. Gibson played all four tests in what was ultimately a series whitewash at the hands of New Zealand. This was a steep learning curve for Gibson, who returned to fly-half for Ireland in the intervening years until the next tour. The experiment to play Gibson at centre was not repeated on yet another dismal Lions tour in 1968, this time to South Africa. It was here that Gibson became the first ever official replacement in rugby history as the rugby authorities caught up with the wisdom of the southern hemisphere teams who had unofficially been replacing injured players for some years. An injury to Barry John necessitated the need for Gibson to play at outside half and that was that – until his own injury later that year led to the rise of Barry McGann and Gibson had to try and force his way back into the Irish set-up. His natural skill and ability were used to plug a gap and Gibson returned at inside centre, where he thrived and earned selection to yet another Lions tour, returning to New Zealand in 1971.

Gibson was the only non-Welsh player to feature in the back line for the first test; lining up alongside Barry John and John Dawes in midfield, supported by the likes of J.P.R. Williams at full-back and Gareth Edwards at scrum-half, they formed perhaps the greatest back line ever assembled, a real selection of superstars, and Gibson was not out of place. His line-breaking ability was paramount to what remains the only victorious Lions tour of New Zealand.

Like many timeless greats, he seemed to age slowly, his talents never waning through his long years. His legs lasted through the decade and a half of punishment and he remained quick to deputise on the wing for four appearances in the 1978 Five Nations Championship, just before retiring. Gibson's most enduring quality, though, was his creativity, his ability to spot what nobody else could: reading the game like an experienced tracker, he was not only able to initiate the most unlikely of moves, but also able to support his teammates in the blink of an eye.

Nothing illustrated this better than the way Gibson was able to slot so seamlessly into the heart of the Welsh-dominated

Lions back line of 1971. Teammates Gareth Edwards, Barry John and J.P.R. Williams were instinctive players, who were able to play the most astonishing rugby. Gibson complemented this beautifully with a more thoughtful, adaptable and intelligent approach. According to the All Blacks captain Colin Meads, the real foundation for that success was provided by Mervyn Davies and Mike Gibson. Gibson's inventiveness stunned the All Blacks; being surrounded by stellar teammates brought out the best in him and showed his potential as a nearly perfect rugby player, able to play in any position.

Anyone who had the fortune of watching Mike Gibson in his prime remembers his exploits fondly. Admired in the southern hemisphere as well as by home nations opposition, Gibson was a delight to spectators and fellow players alike, a glowing talent that remained magnificent for Ireland for a full fifteen years. His name will forever be associated with all that is great about Irish rugby.

29. JASON LEONARD

Prop, England 1990–2004

Jason 'The Fun Bus' Leonard had a lengthy career, surviving and thriving through the transition from the amateur game into professionalism in a way that no other England player managed. Leonard was one of the most skilful and intelligent prop forwards in the game and this, combined with his level of commitment, meant he was able to adapt constantly; he was a key player in the England set-up for well over a decade.

Making his debut against Argentina in 1990, Leonard cut a striking figure. Donning a headband with his sleeves rolled up, his appearance matched his approach: strong and impressive. Although he bulked up in later years to a behemoth size in order to withstand the modern scrum, Leonard began his career as a ferocious but mobile prop.

Leonard was still a very raw player by the time of the World Cup in 1991, but was part of a formidable front row, alongside Brian Moore and opposite Jeff Probyn; England's dominant scrum was relied upon for much of the team's success. Losing to the All Blacks in the group stages before recovering to squeak past Scotland in the semi-final, England lost to Australia in the final and the disappointment was huge for the young prop forward. The ability to recover and keep his emotions level would play a key part in Leonard's development as a Five Nations grand slam win over Wales the next spring was followed by a horrific spinal injury.

Following a successful operation, Leonard's rehabilitation was faster than anticipated, thanks not least to his immense mental strength. Despite a bone-grafting operation, Leonard returned to action after only seven months out and was rewarded with selection for the Lions tour of 1993.

Leonard was to participate in three Lions tours in his career. He played his part in famous test victories over New Zealand in 1993 and later Australia in 2001, ultimately losing both series. But it was against the Springboks in 1997 that he was first utilised to great impact off the bench.

As Leonard's career progressed, he acquired the skills to play at both loosehead and tighthead prop; although loosehead remained his preferred position, he was able to provide coaches with much-desired flexibility. It also made him very difficult to drop from the squad and he was ever-present for many years. After injury niggles started to affect

his mobility, Leonard began to bulk up and work hard on his conditioning. This physicality certainly helped him with the transition into the professional game, and one would be forgiven for believing that his nickname came from his driving into the scrum with the power of a bus, or even making a tackle with such strength. Leonard, though, will admit that the origin of the nickname is far less flattering – after piling on some weight following an injury, a teammate said that he looked like a big London bus while wearing the red England training jersey. Although the nickname stuck, Leonard could not be accused of neglecting his physical conditioning; his stamina and longevity, and the vast number of international appearances, disprove that entirely.

What made Leonard one of the greatest prop forwards – if not the greatest loosehead of all time – was his intelligence. It's small wonder that as the years mounted up, so did the frequency of his appearances as a replacement. He was able to read the scrum and the technique of the opposition and able to make a devastating impact to any fatigued front row. Despite spending a large proportion of his time without the ball, Leonard is an unsung hero, having an even greater impact as his years progressed.

By the time the World Cup rolled around in 2003, Leonard was 35 and the only player remaining from the 1991 squad, but he remained a vital part of England's front row. And although his stamina wasn't quite up to the intensity of participating in every minute of the World Cup campaign, he did feature in every game, most often as a replacement, but also making some starting appearances. Most crucial, of course, was the huge impact he made off the bench in the final against Australia.

The scrum was a key part of England's game plan in 2003 and at the start of the game, the front row were tearing the

Aussies to pieces. But their aggression got the better of them and as the scrums were collapsing and wheeling, the referee started penalising England. This was catastrophic, but listening to the referee on the replacements bench was Jason Leonard. The Fun Bus arrived on the pitch after normal time was over, with the scores level. Any slip-up in the scrum would gift Australia three points, and cost England the World Cup. Jason spoke with the referee and the England pack rallied to their experienced prop. The scrum instantly stabilised and England were able to control the game once again. The impact that Leonard had from the bench in that final is not to be underestimated. Jason Leonard racked up a few more England games following that World Cup and retired after the 2004 Six Nations as England's most capped player of all time.

28. GEORGE NEPIA

Full-back, New Zealand 1925–30

In more than 100 years of New Zealand rugby, from the Originals to the World Cup-retaining Richie McCaw era, the All Blacks have never had another player manage a statistical feat that even comes close to matching what George Nepia achieved, nor had a team that has quite been able to live up to that which became known in the 1924/25 tour as the 'Invincibles'.

The Invincibles played 30 matches in Europe and two in Canada over the space of six months and won every single one of them. What was even more remarkable was that

nineteen-year-old George Nepia played full-back in every game – and as these were the days long before replacements were introduced, Nepia played in every minute of that long tour. A staggering feat of physical endurance in itself, and although he played along other legendary All Blacks, such as Maurice and Cyril Brownlie, Mark Nicholls and Bert Cooke, Nepia was the face of the tour and his name has endured as a symbol of Maori rugby.

Nepia was not the first Kiwi to lead the Haka; in fact the All Blacks have been performing the ritual for as long as they have been playing international rugby. But during that tour, Nepia helped bring fame to the traditional dance by performing it after the national anthem in front of crowds on the other side of the world. This 'weird chant' was a source of curiosity to the spectators from the home nations. Newspapers at the time were full of references to the 'famous war dance', led by George Nepia.

Aside from his clear natural talent, innate composure and incredible athletic technique, Nepia had a very strong physical presence for a full-back of this era. Although only five foot nine, he was stocky and weighed in at around thirteen stone. This wasn't much less than the forwards of this era and it meant he was fearless and imposing in defence. In the days when, alongside defence, kicking to touch was a full-back's primary job, he had a great technique for kicking out of hand.

Nepia was a huge star in the eyes of the British press at the time, leaving the journalists in awe. Superlatives were heaped upon him with universal praise; it was often agreed that Nepia was the greatest full-back in history.

This should have been the springboard for a long and successful career, but prejudices in South Africa and his Maori ancestry meant that he and half-back Jimmy Mill were declared ineligible for the 1928 tour on racial grounds. During this time, Nepia kept a small farm on the remote East Coast, adding to his outcast reputation. This remoteness had led to confusion before: he was excluded from the Maori tour of Great Britain in 1926/27, possibly due to logistical issues. Nepia then missed the 1929 tour of Australia due to injury. In fact, the only full series Nepia participated in after the 'Invincibles' series was against the touring British & Irish Lions side in 1930, and this was to be the last time he played for the All Blacks.

Nepia's farm suffered greatly during the Great Depression and for financial reasons he decided to switch codes and leave his family behind in 1935 and play for the short-lived Streatham & Mitcham RLFC in England, before moving to Halifax. This decision to switch to league saw him cast out from rugby union.

The separation from his young family – a wife and four children – took its toll on Nepia and he returned just two years later to play for Manukau Magpies and even turned out for the New Zealand rugby league side during this time.

New Zealand rugby union held an amnesty in 1947, allowing league players a route back to union if they chose to and Nepia was reinstated to the world of rugby union aged 41. He played sporadically for the East Coast side Olympiads before playing his last game in 1950 against Poverty Bay, a team captained by his eldest son, also named George. At 44, George Snr became the oldest player to feature in a first-class match, and it remains the only instance of first-class rugby in New Zealand where a father and a son have played against each other.

Despite having been unavailable or ineligible for many years, Nepia still ended his career having played 46 times for the All Blacks. Most of these were during his extraordinary feat as a teenager, giving a touch of romanticism to Nepia's career. His status as an idol was confirmed when the New Zealand postal service put his face on a stamp in 1990, four years after his death at age 81. Many documentaries and books have added to the legend of Nepia, ensuring that his name and status live on through future generations.

27. FRIK DU PREEZ

Lock, South Africa 1961–71

He was versatile long before it was essential, and before it was even fashionable. Frik du Preez was the rarest of beasts: a lock who was as comfortable clearing bodies out of rucks and making hits as he was kicking for goal.

Du Preez was an excellent all-round footballer, and like the Australian lock John Eales in the generation that would follow, he was that original phenomenon: the fascinating sight of lock that could kick. What's more surprising is that although he was a tower of strength in the lineout, he was not particularly tall. He also had a fantastic turn of pace, and fine running skills with ball in hand, as he showed in the try he scored against the British Lions in 1968.

It feels like a mistake in the records that there is only one try to du Preez's international record – but it was some try. In the first test against the 1968 Lions, Frik du Preez peeled around the front of a lineout from just outside his own 22-yard line and, with the ball tucked under his arm (in a somewhat iconic image), charged all cylinders along the touchline leaving, among others, Gareth Edwards in his wake. Now only Lions full-back Tom Kiernan stood in front of him but throughout Kiernan's whole career, he had never looked so vulnerable. He may as well have tried to stop a locomotive going at full speed. Frik scored the try and the Springboks won the tightly fought encounter.

Du Preez is truly revered by the passionate South African fans, and many call him their country's greatest ever player. In many ways that accolade takes into account more than du Preez's performances on the field, also reflecting his charisma and influence on those around him, despite a fierce attitude on the pitch.

South Africa have always had a reputation for tough tackles and physical bullying of their opponents and for all of his technical ability, du Preez was no exception. Known to make the occasional knockout blow in tackles that would be illegal by today's standards, he had the ability to shake a team's confidence and win crucial games.

The embodiment of this came in New Zealand's famous tour of South Africa in 1970, when four minutes into the game du Preez managed to concuss New Zealand's key man Chris Laidlaw with a shuddering double tackle. It wasn't the heaviest tackle of the day; that accolade went to Joggie Jansen only minutes later. (Jansen's crash tackle effectively removed another key player from the match, as Wayne Cottrell was left unconscious and never really recovered that day. In fact, the turnover directly led to a South African try.)

Du Preez led by example; he set a precedent that his team was able to follow. By less than pretty means, they had overcome a significant challenge after New Zealand arrived in 1970 all fired up. After the controversies over South Africa's racist policies that marred the 1960 tour, New Zealand had had an extensive set of warm-up matches where they utterly dominated every team they came up against.

This led the media to speculate if they could emulate the famous 'Invincibles' team of 1924/25. Frik du Preez's South Africa met this challenge head on, defeating New Zealand in three of the four tests – indeed the only test South Africa lost was by one point. This domination over New Zealand has never really been repeated since, by any nation.

For many years du Preez held the record for the most test matches played for South Africa, with 38 appearances (along with the excellent flanker Jan Ellis). Although this was before South Africa's international exile, there were far fewer tests and du Preez was a true icon for more than a generation of South African rugby fans.

South African rugby is rich with true personalities and characters that have undoubtedly had a huge impact on the game worldwide. There's no denying the importance of rugby to the nation of South Africa, and their history is littered with memorable greats. Among these is Frik du Preez, the archetypal rugby player and, for many, the true embodiment of the sport.

26. SERGE BETSEN

Flanker, France 1997–2007

Almost universally acclaimed as one of the elite loose forwards of the professional era, Serge Betsen is revered as one of the most ferocious players to ever play for Les Bleus, as well as for his warmth and charisma off the pitch.

Although he made his debut against Italy in 1997, he did not play again for France until he was 25, when he emerged as a standout player in the 2000 Six Nations Championship. He quickly consolidated his place in the national side and played at the highest level for France until he was 36, a remarkable age for someone who has taken (and dealt out) the level of physical punishment that he did.

Betsen was able to play on both flanks of the scrum with equal proficiency. He was a strong runner with the ball, often able to carry the ball into the most stubborn of defences and make precious yards breaking through the gain line. But it was for his tackling for which he would be remembered. Not simply the strength with which he was able to hit and drive the opposition back, but his outstanding work rate. At one point, the French national side claimed that Betsen was breaking records for the most tackles made in international tests. Although unverified, such claims were difficult to refute. Betsen seemed unrelenting and was dogged in his defensive work.

Betsen was at his destructive best when he was given free rein to hunt down the opposition playmakers. He provided turnover ball for France through huge hits and relentless foraging in the rucks. Not only that, through sheer physical dominance, he was able to entirely man-mark players out of a game.

Few will remember this better than Jonny Wilkinson, who in 2002 was the best number ten in the world. Betsen was able to humiliate Wilkinson, forcing his early replacement. This was no easy feat, and was not a case of physical bullying, for Wilkinson was one of the toughest fly-halves out there, built like a back row himself. Betsen managed it through speed and positional savvy; he demoralised Wilkinson by preventing him from playing the game he wanted to play, rendering him ineffectual. He was unremitting in his pursuit of Jonny and Clive Woodward himself admitted that

England had been beaten single-handedly by the French back row. France went on to win the grand slam and Betsen was named France's International Player of the Year.

In what was a highly contested repeat fixture in the 2003 World Cup semi-final, Betsen again made life incredibly difficult for England, but France were unable to stop the eventual champions, with Betsen scoring the only try in a hard-fought 24-7 loss.

Betsen was renowned as a fearless tackler, and this physicality had an effect on his body. He missed the 2005 autumn internationals after fracturing his cheekbone in a match against Toulouse. Despite such setbacks, he continued with his selfless and intimidating approach. In the 2007 Six Nations Championship, which France won, he made more tackles than any other player in the tournament. In fact, Betsen's career corresponded with a real bright period for Les Bleus; in the eight tournaments that Betsen participated in, France won four outright, including two grand slams.

The type of player that can individually have a colossal impact on spectators, rare in any case, is more often found among the backs. It's far more common to find a winger or full-back who can turn the game on its head with a strong counter-attack. But Betsen helped prove that you can find a back-row forward with the ability to lift the team and supporters on his shoulders with hit after hit, simultaneously disrupting the opposition and encouraging his teammates.

Serge was in superb form just before his retirement in 2007, and his finest game since 2002 came in the quarter-final of that year's World Cup and that famous win against strong tournament favourites New Zealand. But the key for Betsen was consistency. He was incredibly consistent over his 63 caps, unlike many of his French contemporaries. France are renowned for their unpredictable form, known to slump to heavy defeats, and yet they always seem the most likely of the northern hemisphere sides to pull a victory out of the bag against the All Blacks. Although teams find it hard to prepare against the erratic Les Bleus, with Betson in the side, you were always guaranteed a tough time.

Although he retired from international rugby almost a decade ago, Serge Betson's impact is still felt. Through his remorseless tackling, Betsen earned himself the nickname 'La Faucheuse', which is often translated as 'the Grim Reaper'. Yet in many ways it does not reflect the true Serge Betsen, an endearingly lively and affable man. Since retiring, as well as many media and punditry appearances, he is well known for his philanthropic work and continues to play in and organise matches while raising money for the Serge Betsen Academy, a charity which promotes health and wellness guidance through rugby clinics for children in Cameroon.

25. SHANE WILLIAMS

Wing, Wales 2000–13

In 2002, Shane Williams nearly quit rugby entirely when, following a series of hamstring injuries, he found himself facing a tough time as Wales' third-choice scrum-half. As much as he would later become known for his quick feet, small stature and a huge number of test tries, Williams was also known for his competitive edge and refusal to quit.

Although Shane Williams is one of the first names people turn to in order to argue against the increasing size and weight of players in the modern game, it's unfair to remember him simply as someone who was great despite his size. The Welsh Wizard was arguably one of the most inspirational players ever to grace this great game. Every kid who was deemed 'too small to play' went straight down the park after seeing Shane Williams pulling on the Welsh jersey.

Everyone remembers his side-stepping magic and a change of pace that left defenders looking as dumbfounded as Wile E. Coyote, but it's easy to forget just how hard Shane Williams worked in order to be able to hold his own physically on the international stage. Having burst on to the scene in exciting fashion, he spent two years in the test wilderness amid concerns over his size.

Williams was awarded his first cap as a replacement against France in the 2000 Six Nations Championship, three weeks short of his 23rd birthday and weighing a little over eleven stone. He scored in his first full start for Wales with a try against Italy in the same tournament. But this wasn't to last. He was unable to hold down a place in the Wales team and it was effectively a false start for Williams' career.

He was taken to the 2003 Rugby World Cup in Australia, but as a third-choice scrum-half. After Wales made a stuttering start to their campaign, recording unimpressive victories against Tonga and Italy, who proved more difficult opponents than the bookies had made out, they had unconvincingly qualified to the knockout stages. Wales were second in their group with only the tournament favourites, the All Blacks, to play. Wales (and future New Zealand) coach Steve Hansen made some interesting line-up changes, deciding to rest ten first-team players who had failed to impress in the earlier games. Wales were expected to lose heavily, and it could be argued that Hansen was protecting these players from humiliation or trying to motivate them by letting them know their place wasn't guaranteed – or even simply trying to prevent injuries against a physically dominant New Zealand side. Whatever Hansen's reasons, it was here that Shane Williams played his first game for Wales in a World Cup, out on the right wing.

The game wasn't quite the one-sided contest that was predicted. Despite the Kiwis taking an early lead, the young and inexperienced Wales team took the game to their intimidating opposition, rarely making mistakes, completing phase after phase and matching the All Blacks in an unexpectedly open game. Lining up against Joe Rokocoko and Doug Howlett, one winger in particular stood out. Sparking a comeback from 28-10 down after half an hour gone, Shane Williams bolted through the centre of the New Zealand pack, setting up a wonderful try with Wales' best rugby of the tournament. And not long after half-time Williams scored the try that took the score to 28-34, the commentator shouting, 'Give it to Williams, he's the man!' New Zealand were sparked into life and although the game finished a misleading 53-37, the resurgent Welsh had shown that the Kiwis were far from indestructible – and Shane Williams had shown himself on the big stage.

Wales were revitalised, and although they were to lose in the quarter-finals to eventual winners England, this kick-started the career of their most potent try scorer of the modern era. Having grabbed his chance at the 2003 World Cup, Williams quickly cemented his position as the first-choice winger, working on his physique and emerging as the greatest Welsh player of his generation.

From there, Williams helped Wales end their 27-year grand slam drought in the Six Nations, where as well as scoring tries against Italy and Scotland, he scored the crucial try in their opening game against the heavily favoured world

champions England, securing a famous 11-9 victory. He was then selected for the British & Irish Lions for their 2005 New Zealand tour, where he equalled a single-game Lions record by scoring five tries in a warm-up match against Manawatu.

But the most successful era for Shane Williams was yet to come. In 2008 Williams helped Wales to yet another Six Nations grand slam victory, ending the tournament as top try scorer and being named player of the tournament. Further recognition came when, that same year, Williams became the first Welshman to be named IRB Player of the Year. Unsurprisingly, Williams was named in the British & Irish Lions squad for the 2009 tour to South Africa. Williams somehow missed out on a starting place in the first two tests as England's Ugo Monye and Ireland's Luke Fitzgerald were selected ahead of him in two narrow defeats for the Lions. With the tour already lost, Williams was selected to play in the final test, where he produced a man-of-the-match performance and scored two tries in the series' only victory over the Springboks.

With Wales losing out to Fiji and never making it out of the group stages of the 2007 World Cup, 2011 was Shane Williams' last chance to shine on the world stage. After losing by only one point to defending champions South Africa in their opening game, Wales romped past Ireland to reach the semi-final, losing 8-9 to France in a hard-fought contest in which many had Wales down as the better side.

Williams was heartbroken, and after stating in interviews that he felt Wales should have won the World Cup, he announced his intention to retire from playing for his country. His final game would be against Australia in December 2011. It was only fitting that he scored a try with the very last touch of his international career, in added time, as the game finished 24-18 to Australia.

Retirement sat about as well with Williams as being told he was too small in the first place, and during the 2013 Lions tour of Australia, where Williams was a commentator, he was invited to play one final game against the ACT Brumbies.

All of the impressive records and statistics that support Williams' claim as one of the greatest players of the game cannot tell the full story. It was the manner in which he played and the era in which he played that truly define the player. Guinness created a whole advertising campaign on his retirement, centred around the fact that Williams was once thought 'too small to play' but was redeemed by the 'strength of his heart'. That is testament to the impact that he had on the game, not just as an inspirational figure but as one of the greatest entertainers rugby has ever seen.

Every fan loves a player who can beat a man with a neat side-step, a winger who can spot a line that nobody else can, one who can change direction with one step and a change of pace that leaves defenders at a standing start. Williams did all of this. Replaced by giant man-mountains George North and Alex Cuthbert – surprisingly agile as they may be – Williams was perhaps the last of a dying breed.

24. RICHARD HILL

Flanker, England 1997–2008

How many times must Richard Hill be called an 'unsung hero' before it is accepted that he is one of the highest-rated players of all time? Perhaps it's the fact that his tally of 71 caps – by no means a small number – still feels like it doesn't do justice to such a dominant player, especially when it's well known that it was injury that stopped him from playing at the highest level for even longer, and not lack of form.

An exceptionally well-rounded player with many aspects to his game, he was often referred to as the 'strong, silent type'. Hill is the only player never to have been dropped during Sir Clive Woodward's England reign. With his prolific work in the rucks and mauls, he suited the style of play that made England such a force. Simply put, Hill was the insurance policy within England's dominant team of the early 2000s, constantly plugging gaps, often first to make a tackle and pouncing on any opportunity to secure a loose ball – the perfect blindside flanker.

Neil Back, although a strong fans' favourite, had been in and out of the England set-up before Woodward's tenure, but the new coach shuffled the back row to suit the Leicester flanker, switching Hill to blindside and Lawrence Dallaglio to number eight. This was the cornerstone to Woodward's vision for a new England, one that would never let the opposition rest, one that forced attacking players into rucks, instantly reducing their threat – and, most crucially, one that forced errors and penalties from which a particularly accurate goal-kicker could create a platform and keep the points ticking over. It all sounded so simple, and the new combination worked as well in practice as it did on paper, Back's impressive speed and sharp reactions and Dallaglio's fierce attacking nature perfectly balanced with Hill's cool reliability and protection.

So well did they work together that it seemed this back row could communicate telepathically. Hill, Back and Dallaglio seemed to hunt like wild animals, bringing a whole new meaning to the term 'pack'. There seemed to be something instinctive in all three that instilled confidence in their teammates.

The reason why Richard Hill was the 'unsung hero' for many was that he was far less flashy than his back-row teammates. He didn't seem to stand out in the same way that Neil Back did, with his distinctive style and appearance, and he didn't quite have the same fierce immediacy as Dallaglio, but it was the unseen work that made critics and teammates purr. Respected by everyone, including the opposition, he was the rugby player's rugby player. Without doing anything flamboyant, he was always winning the ball back or making that tackle or scoring that try.

For a player to be consistently in the right place at the right time, both in defence and in attack, shows a high level of understanding. Hill's intelligence meant that he knew where the danger would come from – he could see the game several rucks ahead and was prepared for any lapse in concentration from his opposition, ready to steal the ball away and allow others to take the glory.

Although it's not a talent unique to Hill, there are few that have been as effective at protecting their backs. By his impeccable positioning and timing, he always seemed able to track the most meandering of runs; he always knew when anyone in the back three was in trouble, and nobody ever seemed to get isolated when Hill was on the pitch.

That's not to say that Hill was not a good ball-carrier himself. As versatile and canny with ball in hand as without, he had incredible stamina. It's impossible to overstate Hill's value to the England squad, which was proven when he wasn't sent home, despite a hamstring injury, on the opening day of the World Cup in 2003.

England had back-row players in the squad – Lewis Moody, Martin Corry, Joe Worsley – who could cover Hill's absence.

Admittedly they were all very different in their style of play from Hill, and it couldn't be said that Woodward didn't have options. With Hill injured, there was also the opportunity to send him home and call up one of the unselected stars (Simon Shaw, Austin Healey and Graham Rowntree were all watching the World Cup from their living rooms). Hill was asked to stay in the hope that he would be ready to play if England reached the semi-final, which they did, somewhat unconvincingly.

The gamble paid off, his return was a visible boost to the entire team and he helped England play their best rugby of the tournament to stroll past France, before playing a key role in the unforgettable World Cup final victory over Australia.

Hill injured the anterior cruciate ligament in his left knee in October 2004, and was out for the following seven months. Despite hardly clocking any playing time that season, he returned to be named in a Lions squad for the third time in 2005. Perhaps he rushed back from injury too soon. Named in the starting XV for the first test against the All Blacks, he suffered a knee injury almost immediately, ending his tour.

For all of Hill's virtues, he is not a player you will often see on highlights reels. His personality when interviewed matched his style of play. There was no hogging the limelight. Uncomfortable with the press, he was more than happy to let the flashier players take the credit.

He was a tough man, and would never back away from a confrontation, but he never seemed to provoke a fight – unlike his replacement Lewis Moody. He played hard and he played fair – unlike his back-row partner Back, who was known for his share of gamesmanship.

Hill never really recovered from his injuries and played his last games with a noticeable limp, which will be with him for the rest of his life. When he finally did retire, he did so with the minimum of fuss. There was no fanfare, no real press conference, but in a manner befitting Richard Hill, there was a slight delay, followed by an outpouring of emotion from critics across the world, talking about how underrated Hill had been throughout his career. For those in the know, he was one of the greatest forwards ever to play for England, and one whom they've never really been able to replace.

Richard Hill has made this list of the greatest rugby players of all time, not out of respect for a player who would have been great were it not for a constant battle with injury; he has made the list for his achievements on the pitch – and would surely be placed higher had he not succumbed to the physical strain that he placed upon his body.

23. JEAN-PIERRE RIVES

Flanker, France 1975–84

Once deemed too small to be an international rugby player, Jean-Pierre Rives became a real cult figure for France as he repeatedly defied expectations and carved his name into the history of rugby.

While it was his technical ability that won him many plaudits from coaches and critics, he endeared himself to supporters with his flair and his gung-ho attitude. Always in the thick of the action, the enduring image of Jean-Pierre Rives is one of his face covered in blood, something which occurred startlingly frequently.

Although he was a small guy, not only did he not shy

away from the action, he actively sought it out. Whether that meant crunching dump tackles on men twice his size, or demonstrating his selflessness by throwing himself into the breakdown, he would energise his team with displays of commitment and audacious activity.

Jean-Pierre Rives was instrumental to the development of French rugby. Playing in a decade dominated by a Wales side the like of which we'll never see again, a sublimely talented French side was overshadowed. Les Bleus in the second half of the 1970s were the only northern hemisphere side who had the ability to go toe-to-toe with the Welsh and many Five Nations Championships of the time were decided either at the Parc des Princes or in Cardiff.

Rives came to epitomise the French side of the time, and as captain saw it as his duty to constantly be in the midst of everything, remaining close to the ball for the full game, in the thick of the action. The side became known as a gloriously entertaining and unpredictable side, fluctuating between success and abject failure, and were never dull – not a million miles away from the current French side. The legacy that endures was laid by Rives. Indeed, a later French hero, Serge Betsen, had a similar tackling style to Rives, one where it seemed like he would genuinely want to tackle straight through the opponent, and although clean and technical, he displayed a real hatred of the attacking player.

Rives played like a man with something to prove. He always stood out on the pitch due to his distinctive appearance; with his long blond hair, he became a firm fans' favourite early in his career. In 1975, Jean-Pierre made his debut aged 22 at Twickenham in France's victory over England. A committed display made an impression and he instantly became a fixture in the French side. Alongside Jean-Claude Skrela and Jean-Pierre Bastiat, Rives managed to form an incredibly impressive back row, founding one of the greatest combinations the game has ever seen. With sheer dominance around the breakdown, they terrorised teams, forcing an open game which suited the Gallic style and taking many more conservative opposition sides out of their comfort zone. The freedom their back row afforded Les Bleus allowed the entire side to play with a vigour and openness rarely seen in the modern game. It was a breathtaking sight for spectators.

A Five Nations grand slam is an impressive feat for any player to be involved in, but in 1978 France achieved only the second in their history – made all the more remarkable by a final victory over a Wales side containing Phil Bennett, J.P.R. Williams and Gareth Edwards to name but a few. The XV who achieved that famous victory over Wales in Paris were the exact same XV who had played in every game of the grand slam; this remains the only time this has happened.

This France team would have dominated for a decade in any other era, but had to relinquish a successive grand slam the following year in the reverse fixture held in Cardiff. This was Jean-Pierre Rives' first season as captain of Les Bleus and facing such world-class opposition was a harsh lesson, but the rivalry pushed both sides to continuous improvement.

Rives also participated in a famous tour of New Zealand, to face the mighty All Blacks. The first test saw the French easily defeated 23-9, but in true tenacious French style, they came out the next week as a side full of confidence and gusto. Rives and his team were more than a match for the All Blacks this time, running the ball at any opportunity, relentlessly testing the defence and scoring four tries to triumph 24-19, with Rives exhibiting all of his ferocity to keep up the pace and flair. Further success followed with another Five Nations grand slam in 1981, following a dramatic 16-12 win at Twickenham.

Again, the grand slam heroics didn't last long as, true to the Gallic erraticism, the next year they only narrowly avoided the wooden spoon, their only victory of the season coming against the in-form Irish, denying them a grand slam in the final game. Following a defeat to minnows Romania in the autumn of 1982, they emerged as joint champions in 1983, sharing the title with the Irish. This hectic form would continue long after Jean-Pierre Rives retired the next season.

Following his retirement from rugby Rives decided to pursue his other passion – art. Although it is an unusual path for a retired sportsman, Rives' sculptures have been exhibited throughout the world. His two passions overlapped in 2007 when he designed the Giuseppe Garibaldi Trophy, awarded each year to the winner of the Six Nations match between France and Italy.

For all his fame and success on the art scene, rugby fans will remember Jean-Pierre Rives as the competitive and furious blood-stained blond hero at the base of the French scrum. An icon for all of those labelled too small to play rugby, he demonstrated that heart and passion mean more than physical presence and natural athleticism – a message that resonates with fans throughout the world.

22. HUGO PORTA

Fly-half, Argentina 1971–90

Argentina in the 21st century have proven themselves to be real contenders on the world rugby stage. However, this is a recent development and before the 1970s Argentina were reliable whipping boys whenever they faced strong opposition. Hugo Porta changed this and proved an exceptional player who lifted an entire nation. As their first truly world-class player, Porta raised the profile of the sport in his country almost single-handedly. He is without doubt one of the most naturally gifted fly-halves the game has ever seen. The fact that he retired aged 39, with his career spanning a remarkable nineteen years, only goes to prove how much Argentina relied on him and how reluctant they were to let him retire.

Porta began his career playing soccer, reportedly training with Boca Juniors before switching to rugby. This background was reflected in his natural and immensely skilful kicking ability. He was able to score a drop-goal with unerring accuracy under intense pressure, as well as showing tactical kicking to win precious yards and positions with finesse.

Hugo Porta was eased into international rugby somewhat, earning his first four caps aged twenty against South American opposition in the form of Chile, Uruguay, Brazil and Paraguay. Argentina won all four of these games, with Porta finding the try line three times, as he was able to experiment in his developmental years. His first taste of world-class opposition followed in the next year as they faced the South Africa Under-23 side. Los Pumas were comprehensively beaten in the first test, but Porta managed to rouse the Argentinian side to a hard-fought 18-16 victory a week later, scoring a try in the process. This was the first glimpse of Porta's nascent quality, and his calm mental process, not being fazed by superior opposition, which complemented his natural gifts.

Through the 1970s, Porta helped Argentina develop and grow from rugby obscurity into a genuinely competitive side, worthy of world-class opposition. Although they were yet

to defeat a major side in a first-class test match, Los Pumas came within seconds of a famous victory over the legendary Wales side at their peak in Cardiff in 1976; the shock was only avoided by a try from the eternal Gareth Edwards and the match finished 20-19. An 18-18 draw with France followed the next year, with Porta responsible for all of his side's points. It was not beautiful free-flowing rugby, certainly not the open style that Argentina impress with today, but it was a stubborn, difficult, physical game, with the mental and physical strength of a united pack establishing their position on the field, relying on Porta to kick them to success.

Argentina played their first ever test against Australia in 1979 and Porta and his Pumas defeated the Wallabies 24-13. The fly-half was once again the talisman and star player as he landed two conversions, three drop-goals and a penalty during the game that put the Argentinian side on the map. After the previous near-misses, this was Porta's first victory against truly world-class opposition.

It's important to remember that it's even more difficult to compare Porta with any other player. He lifted an entire nation on his shoulders and there has never been a side where one player has stood so much further ahead than any other. Hugo Porta is truly unique in his status as a world great without ever coming close to winning a major competition or even tour series.

During South Africa's international isolation, they were struggling for competitive sides to face. Porta played a part in a touring side named the South American Jaguars, made up primarily of Argentinian players but not officially recognised, to get around the prohibition of test matches against apartheid South Africa. Porta led this side who managed the impressive feat of defeating the Springboks on their home soil, kicking all 21 of their points. It would not be until 2015 that Argentina would record their first official victory over the Bokke.

In their history, Argentina have never recorded a single test victory against the All Blacks, despite their continual improvement (to the point where a test victory against South Africa or Australia would raise few eyebrows), and in fact they have never came as close as they did with Hugo Porta in 1985, when they secured a 21-21 draw. Once again, Porta scored every single one of Los Pumas' points that day, with a determined pack shutting down New Zealand's attack and Porta himself so close to kicking the Argentines to what would have been the most unlikeliest of victories. Such was Porta's acclaim in his native Argentina that he was awarded their Sportsman of the Year award later that year. Considering the status of rugby union at the time compared to football, this was no small achievement. A generation of young Argentines were looking to Porta as their new hero as he led them to the inaugural World Cup in 1987. Although they managed a solitary victory against Italy, Porta was by then 36 years old, and past his prime.

At the end of the tournament, Porta announced his retirement from rugby, but such was his importance that they truly struggled without him and he was called out of retirement for a tour of the British Isles and three further tests against England, Ireland and Scotland in 1990, all of which were lost. It was to be another five years before their next world-class player was to appear, in the form of Agustín Pichot, who, along with an almighty pack, was able to compete with some world-class opposition. Many more would follow later, but it all began with Hugo Porta, the first Argentinian rugby hero.

21. WILLIE JOHN McBRIDE

Lock, Ireland 1962–75

Although he played 63 times for Ireland in a thirteen-year international career, and rivals Keith Wood as Ireland's greatest ever captain, Willie John McBride is remembered just as fondly throughout all of the home nations for his triumphs with the British & Irish Lions, with whom he toured five times and played in seventeen tests.

Remarkably, McBride did not pick up a rugby ball until he was seventeen. Unlike many of his contemporaries, there was no illustrious schoolboy career to look back upon. But by the time he was 21 he was already a full international, making an astonishing declaration as a real new talent for the world of rugby.

Although he had to play nine tests before tasting a single victory with the Lions, he was a key member of two of the most successful tours in their history – New Zealand in 1971 and South Africa in 1974.

In the famous '71 series victory against the All Blacks he was pack leader, matching their opponents and allowing the genius of Edwards and John to enjoy the possession they needed to secure victory.

McBride was made captain for the '74 tour following the incredible success in New Zealand. Their squad had great experience: Edwards, JPR, J.J. Williams to name but a few. But a team full of individuals would quickly be found out against a well-drilled, physical and talented South Africa side. A Lions team needed more; it needed McBride to bring them all together. The tour was an unprecedented success.

They didn't just beat the Springboks, it was a comprehensive victory. The back line ran rampant, but McBride along with the outstanding Gordon Brown made up the engine room at the heart of that pack, which more than matched this powerful South Africa side.

An inimitable character, McBride claimed he never went anywhere without his pipe except on to the pitch. This easy-going persona was disarming and presented him as somewhat of an enigma. Although McBride had a reputation as an affable and gracious man, he was formidable on the pitch, especially on that 1974 tour with the infamous '99 call', a signal for the Lions which simply meant 'one in, all in'.

The '99 call' was created in response to the whitewash 1966 tour, a painful memory for the veteran McBride. During the provincial warm-up games on that tour, many star players for the Lions were injured after seemingly being made a target for particularly physical play. The tour was a disaster for the Lions. The South Africa side were superior, but many Lions spectators and players felt that there wasn't a level playing field. McBride wanted to make sure that didn't happen again and in the dressing room before the first warm-up game in '74 he gave the instruction that if anybody was the victim of any unsportsmanlike play, then the call would be made and it would be the duty of every Lions player to go in hard on the nearest Springbok player. In the days before citing and video replay, the logic was that the referee couldn't send every player off – the reasoning was sound, if not a little unsavoury.

They only had to do it once; the genius of the call was to create the myth. Sure enough, after a lineout, early in the first game, there was a seemingly intentional late tackle on Edwards. The call was made and the quick burst of violence meant that not only would this team refrain from any funny

business, but the word spread and they could concentrate on playing rugby.

Although it was during the latter part of his career that McBride found fame with the Lions, he had made an impact and learned valuable lessons early on, bringing at least relative success to the rugby nation of Ireland, who were themselves in a fallow period, notably their first ever win against the Springboks in 1965 and beating Australia in Sydney – the first time any home nation had defeated a southern hemisphere team in their own country. But this form could not be repeated in the Five Nations tournament, and McBride's Ireland never found success against rival home nations.

His skill took him far, but it was the mental strength of McBride that makes him one of Ireland's true greats. At a time when the home nations were better than their southern hemisphere counterparts and when the Welsh were running rampant, McBride was the natural leader. Inspirational and aspirational – during this time, when Five Nations Championships could not be completed due to the Troubles (teams would not travel to play in Dublin), McBride, as an Ulsterman and captain of Ireland, was subject to many death threats, which he did not allow to interrupt his game, and he certainly minimised the effect on his players.

A true athlete, McBride was more than competent in the lineout. His real talent lay in his ability to stay calm, no matter what the pressure was against him. Even when playing against the great Colin Meads, McBride rarely lost a lineout and would always supply great ball to his scrum-half.

It's said that the greatest players are able to lift those around them and allow them to fulfil their potential. McBride was certainly one of those players – a truly unique character that brought the sport to life. Never before was there anyone quite like Willie John McBride, and indeed there has been none since.

20. COLIN MEADS

Lock, New Zealand 1957–71

A hard-nosed and menacing physical player, Colin Meads exemplifies an entire era of rugby union. Nicknamed 'Pinetree' more for his perceived presence than his height, Meads was a hard and unforgiving player, one whose style, if not his stature, was befitting of the nickname.

The leader of a team who utterly dominated world rugby in the 1960s, leading from the pack, Meads – much like the more recent All Blacks captain Richie McCaw – played with a ferocity that showed little regard for his opposition. This legendary global figure built his reputation over his fourteen years at the pinnacle of world rugby as a leader who demonstrated the utmost commitment to winning at all costs. Sometimes this meant a physical, or strictly 'not in the rules of the game' approach, but Meads was no slow-witted thug, and indeed, having started his career in the back row, was one of the more mobile lock forwards of the time.

Meads showed his versatility early in his career. He made his international debut on the 1957 tour to Australia, where he played in all eight warm-up games and both international tests, lining up in the back row. However, he famously scored his first international try on that tour while providing cover on the wing as a teammate was receiving treatment on the sidelines.

Meads was a formidable presence on the field. A real athlete with massive farmyard hands, he would charge the pitch with the ball in one hand, side-stepping opponents with deceptive footwork and throwing dummies; the style of play that New Zealand are famous for now, Meads was playing 50 years ago. Forwards with those levels of handling ability and the ability to offload in the tackle are still coveted assets in today's game, but in the '60s these qualities marked Meads out as one of the best players in the world.

By 1959, and following their series victory over the British & Irish Lions touring side, Meads was an established member of the All Blacks side, although still being shifted between the back row and lock. Once he was settled at lock in 1961, they would remarkably lose only two test matches with Meads in the side over the next nine years (and in fact, one of those losses came when he was playing not in the second row but at number eight, against Australia in 1964).

This absolute perfection in the second row was the result of a wonderful combination of looming natural strength and astute tactical awareness. His tendency on the field to lead by example makes it no coincidence that the era of Pinetree coincides exactly with one of New Zealand's most successful periods. With Meads alongside the likes of Kel Tremain, Ken Gray and later Brian Lochore, the All Blacks had a formidable pack. They were never really in danger of losing any of their tours: not that of Britain, Ireland and France in 1963, nor when they faced the touring sides of Australia and South Africa in 1964 and '65. All of this before a complete whitewash of a touring British & Irish Lions side in 1966.

There is one inescapable blemish on the record of Colin Meads. In 1968 he ended the career of the great Australian scrum-half Ken Catchpole in a horrific incident where he grabbed the half-back's leg in a ruck lifting him off the ground while his other leg remained trapped, tearing his ligaments. While this was an intentional act in and of itself, Meads maintains that the injury was not intentional, and it says more for Catchpole that he insists that there are no hard feelings. This unpleasant incident aside, Meads' off-the-field persona otherwise indicates that he is a warm and kind-hearted gentleman and indeed expends a lot of effort and time as an excellent ambassador for the sport.

But injuries of his own were to dampen the end to Meads' career. At 34, in the first match of a tour to South Africa, Meads fractured his arm. When receiving treatment, it was suggested that there was a slight possibility that it might only be a trapped nerve and his arm might not be broken, so he returned to the pitch in considerable pain to complete the game. South Africa were still able to win the game and the series comfortably against an All Blacks side that missed Meads considerably.

Even with an injury like that at such a stage in his career, Meads did recover and returned to captain an inexperienced All Blacks team to their only series loss against the Lions. Most of the stars of the '60s had already retired and although Meads was hanging on, it looked as though his New Zealand career would now be over. A serious back injury, the result of a car accident, later that year, confirmed the end.

This less than glorious finale did not diminish Meads' legacy or the way he is revered by the New Zealand faithful. Meads' skills and decade of dominance is what he is remembered for. Even when he coached the unauthorised Cavaliers tour to apartheid South Africa in 1986, he was only temporarily excluded and was re-elected to the New Zealand Rugby Union council a few years later.

In many ways, Meads typified a bygone era, not just for New Zealand, but for rugby in general. He was a shrewd player, and those who suggest that perhaps the players from that era may not have survived in the modern game perhaps underestimate Meads' ability to adapt to the game and the opponents he faced. In that way, Meads is the 20th-century Richie McCaw – someone who pushed the laws of the game, manipulating and working on the boundaries to his advantage. It may not always have been pretty, but the New Zealand side in the days of Colin Meads almost always won.

19. GEORGE GREGAN

Scrum-half, Australia 1994–2007

Remembered for his quick hands, small stature (he was just five foot eight) and loud mouth, this World Cup-winning captain is one of the greatest half-backs to ever play the game of rugby. His distribution was outstanding, his audacity was incomparable (for good or ill) and his leadership qualities make him deserving of his position inside the top twenty greatest players of all time.

Although he'd earned his debut against Italy earlier that year, Gregan truly announced his arrival on to the international scene in the 1994 Bledisloe Cup. A match-winning tackle in the dying seconds of the game prevented fierce rivals New Zealand from claiming the prized trophy. Gregan appeared from nowhere to make a spectacular tackle on Jeff Wilson as the All Blacks wing was diving for the line. Gregan's flash of inspiration helped Australia win the Bledisloe Cup that year and is remembered as one of the greatest moments in the Wallabies–All Blacks rivalry. It is one of the more remarkable finales in the competition's history and a moment for which Gregan will be forever remembered and adored Down Under.

When interviewed about what became known as 'that tackle', Gregan said that he could make that tackle a hundred times and Wilson would not spill the ball again. This modesty is surprising, as it is not something usually associated with Gregan, and also seems to be quite misplaced.

In one of his last international tests, he performed yet another try-saver against England in Melbourne. Although it was of less importance, it was even more miraculous. This time he managed to hold Iain Balshaw up after a beautifully cheeky little chip through the Australian line made it look as though placing the ball to the ground for an English try seemed to be a mere formality. In fact, upon first viewing it looks like a clear-cut try. Even watching slow-motion replays, it's difficult to see quite how the little Aussie managed to wrap himself around Balshaw and get his arm between the ball and the ground. This was a magnificent show of strength and sheer determination that once again prevented a try.

A player who straddled the end of the amateur and the beginning of the professional era, Gregan represented a new breed of player – one who played to win and not just for the love of the game. His attitude never failed to divide fans; he was known to taunt opponents on the pitch in a manner that some viewed as boastful. One of his most infamous moments came after the defeat of favourites New Zealand in the 2003 World Cup semi-final; he shouted, 'Four more years boys, four more years'. Safe to say, this did little to endear him to opposition (and indeed many neutral) fans. Despite this, Gregan was at the forefront of many famous Wallabies victories and is respected throughout the rugby world for his leadership, shrewd tactics and an unrelenting desire for victory.

The first time Gregan tasted defeat in the green and gold jersey was in the 1995 World Cup quarter-finals: the 25-22 loss to England. Australia were one of the favourites for the tournament and for a player with such self-belief as Gregan, the unexpected defeat resonated and the hurt only fuelled his desire to impress on the world stage.

The 1999 World Cup may have been less dramatic in its build-up than its 1995 predecessor, but on the pitch it was no less enthralling. Following two successful years as captain following the retirement of John Eales in 1997, Gregan led Australia to the 1999 World Cup, scoring a try against hosts Wales in the quarter-final and playing an integral role in a momentous encounter with the champions South Africa in a semi-final that was won by a drop-goal in extra-time. Gregan became a World Cup-winning captain after seeing off France, who were completely dominated by a comfortable Australian team.

He did lead Australia to another final in their attempt to retain the World Cup in 2003, on the way kicking a drop-goal against Ireland in their pool match and scoring a try against Scotland in the quarter-finals. Gregan stood out and led by example in what was a talented Australian team who managed to defeat the old enemy the All Blacks in the semi-final, only to lose in dramatic fashion to England in the final.

As successful as his record was against the All Blacks, England appeared to be his bogey team. Following jibes that he watched footage of the England team's allegedly boring tactics (which relied heavily on a kicking strategy) in order to fall asleep, he was unable to add another World Cup-winners medal to his collection when England's Jonny Wilkinson kicked the winning drop-goal in a thrilling extra-time final in Sydney.

Blessed with a healthy body for most of his career, which seems like a miracle when you take into account his size and the physicality of the modern game, Gregan is the most capped Australian of all time, surely a demonstration of his physical conditioning as well as his indisputable technical ability.

Following the 2007 Rugby World Cup, in which he only played a minor role, he had somewhat of an Indian summer with French side Toulon, helping the club win promotion back to the Top 14 before a swansong with Suntory Sungoliath in Japan. He finally hung up the boots and called it a day on what was an epic career in 2011, aged 38.

18. BARRY JOHN

Fly-half, Wales 1966–72

Although Barry 'The King' John's playing career was remarkably short, he was the most iconic fly-half of the amateur era, even more influential than the legendary Argentinian idol Hugo Porta. He was so revered that in some corners of Wales, when someone referred to 'The King', it was understood that they were not talking about Elvis Presley. It was precisely this kind of fame that cut John's career short as he decided to retire early, away from the media circus that was developing around his life.

But rightly, it's his exploits on the pitch for which he is remembered. There have been many talented players occupy the outside half position for Wales over the years, but you'll struggle to find anyone who could match Barry

John's phenomenal punting game; he could place the ball with unerring accuracy and he could do it every time. Even with absurd levels of consistency, he was feared by opposition defences as an unpredictable opponent.

It is near impossible to compare the abilities that John demonstrated with those of the modern fly-half greats such as Jonny Wilkinson and Dan Carter, for many reasons – not least because the improvement in the quality of the pitches has meant that Carter and Wilkinson never had to handle the levels of slime on the ball that John had to take into account to make perfectly weighted kicks. And taking into account the technical advances that the ball itself has gone through makes the things that Barry John could do seem all the more remarkable. All of this before mentioning the amateur nature of the game in John's day. Famously both Wilkinson and Carter spend hours every single day practising and perfecting their kicks. It's an entirely pointless discussion, but it would be fascinating to see how the likes of Barry John would perform in the modern game with all of the perks that we now enjoy. What is for certain is that John stood head and shoulders above his contemporaries using little more than innate talent and a faultless instinct.

It was not immediately clear that Wales had a new superstar when Barry John made his international debut against Australia in the winter of 1966 as a surprise replacement for the established David Watkins, who was fatigued after leading the Lions in their tour Down Under. Wales lost this first game, with John under some criticism for a poor performance against an experimental Australian side. He was far from an established player, and in the 1967 Five Nations Championship, John played on an injury and was subsequently dropped after one game; Wales finished last in the competition, a single victory against the old enemy

England, with Watkins at outside half, being the only consolation. Only in John's performances with Llanelli were people able to see the genius lying dormant.

This first year with Wales saw Barry John playing in an inconsistent side that did not bring out the best of his abilities, but as David Watkins departed, dramatically switching codes for league, Wales had little option but to stick with John. An even more influential factor in the rise of Barry John was the partnership he was to form with his scrum-half.

Following two years in the Wales set-up, John was selected for the 1968 Lions tour to South Africa, but a broken collarbone ended his tour after only the first test. It was during his recovery time that he first began playing alongside Gareth Edwards at Cardiff, sowing the seeds for one of the most famous half-back partnerships in rugby history. Grant Fox and David Kirk, Nick Farr-Jones and Michael Lynagh, Ken Catchpole and Phil Hawthorne – rugby union has been blessed by many great partnerships, but few have been as effective and certainly none as significant and iconic as the partnership between John and Edwards.

John's return to international rugby from injury was as part of a Wales team that would dominate northern hemisphere rugby during the 1970s. The team was filled with stars: Edwards, J.P.R. Williams, Gerald Davies and John Dawes to name but a few – an incredible back line filled with an abundance of talent the like of which the world has never seen again. But at the centre of it all was that half-back partnership.

John was at his most dangerous when receiving the tremendous long pass of Edwards. John was able to match his game accordingly, taking on the first-phase defence with his sensational footwork or playing further out and playing it through the hands, unleashing his centres with prophetic

precision. Or, his best weapon, deceiving the defence with his precise and shrewd kicking.

A languid runner who relied more on brains than physical brawn, John laid the foundations for the future innovator Mark Ella. With Gareth Edwards as the provider, John had the time to analyse the play and was able to frustrate the defence with an incredible instinct.

This partnership set the 1971 Five Nations Championship alight, resulting in a Welsh grand slam, and in that same year John was selected for another Lions tour, this time to New Zealand.

It was during this tour that John made the impact which launched him into legendary status. Of all the stars in that famous tour, John shone brightest. His display of tactical kicking in the first test terrorised the reputable All Blacks full-back Fergie McCormick; it was a masterclass in control that set the tone for the rest of the series. In fact, this display was so clinical that even after one test, the All Blacks were panicked, and had to make their selection based upon the threat that John posed. McCormick was dropped for the remainder of the series.

Not that it made much difference. In the third test, John scored what was arguably his most famous try, dummying a drop-goal attempt before waltzing through to score under the posts in front of an astonished Wellington crowd.

John left New Zealand having scored 30 of the Lions' 48 points over the four test matches. That squad remains the only touring Lions side to record a series victory against New Zealand.

In 1972, only a year after returning from the Lions tour, Barry John retired from rugby at just 27 years of age. He claimed that the expectations and pressures being placed on him by his country and the media were too much to handle.

This was the televised age, yet union was still an amateur game. He was the most recognisable star, without the advice and structure (and pay) in place to handle it.

Wales still continued to dominate throughout the '70s even without Barry John. Gareth Edwards was given a more than capable replacement in the incredible Phil Bennett, whose talent was almost enough to make this list himself. But the superior power to govern that Barry John possessed laid the foundations for this Wales side, who had collected one of the greatest groups of players the sport will likely ever see.

After his retirement John all but vanished from the public eye. His ability on the pitch and the majesty of his control of a game of rugby meant that he was a one-off in the eyes of Welsh fans and he was sorely missed by the rugby community.

17. DANIE GERBER

Centre, South Africa 1980–92

Few are in any doubt that without the political shadow cast over South Africa during the years in which he played, Danie Gerber would have proven himself one of the most gifted midfield players to ever grace the game. The mere 24 caps to his name in the record books are an incredibly misleading figure.

It's sometimes more difficult than it should be to disassociate politics from international sport; the two are so often intertwined. International tests are widely touted as metaphors by the press and commentators. And in the history of rugby, there has been no more striking and controversial example of this than the relationship between South Africa's rugby union team of the 1980s and the politics of that nation.

Danie Gerber was a vastly talented centre, whose career was inhibited and overshadowed by apartheid. This despised regime severely limited Gerber, who was only able to represent South Africa in the northern hemisphere three times and who only played one test match against Australia. Although many spectators were robbed of the pleasure of seeing this great man in action, those that did see him play consider him one of the best players ever to play the game.

Evaluating from a purely rugby perspective, Danie Gerber is quite probably the greatest centre ever to play for the Springboks. He was physically huge and an incredibly powerful runner. The gulf in quality between him and his nearest opponent was staggering; he was a man born to score tries, playing among mere mortals. From broken play, few have been able to demolish a defence in the same way as Gerber. Flawless footwork and an ability to side-step either way without losing pace kept defenders guessing and paved the way for Gerber to score some of the most breathtaking individual tries the game will likely ever see. It was not just his speed and footwork: Gerber had that rare combination of size and strength alongside his agility. This made him as rock-solid in defence as he was potent in attack, where he was frequently to break through tackles. This made him a real crowd favourite and he is fondly remembered by Springboks fans as the most exciting player they have ever had.

Gerber's first cap came in 1980 against the touring South American Jaguars, scoring a try on his debut. Gerber went on to make fifteen test appearances before the international community imposed restrictions barring South Africa from test rugby so long as apartheid remained. He scored an impressive fourteen tries in those matches, including two in a hard-fought victory over Ireland in 1981. But after a steep learning curve in a losing tour to New Zealand in 1981 where Gerber didn't find the try line once, the young centre improved astronomically for South Africa in the years preceding their exclusion.

England were the only northern hemisphere side to face Gerber approaching his peak. He had faced both the Irish and the French before, but in 1984 Gerber was lethal, scoring four tries in two tests against the English with one superb solo effort in front of a rapturous home-town crowd in Port Elizabeth. But perhaps his finest moment was an eighteen-minute hat-trick in the second test as South Africa recorded a then-record 35-9 win over England at Ellis Park.

The only time that Gerber played in the northern hemisphere was for the invitational side Barbarians in 1983, when they faced Scotland at Murrayfield. The Barbarians won 33-17, with Gerber making a standout performance and scoring two tries. Gerber had quite an impact on the rugby critics and journalists at the time and much was made of his devastating straight-line direct running. It was not simply brainless; he was able to draw defenders in, and even when not scoring himself, he opened his back line up and gave them many more options.

The stage was set for an illustrious career, but then came those wilderness years. Gerber became the most famous and revered player in the South African club game but could go no further. Making nearly 200 club appearances, he kept a strict fitness regime throughout and his physical dominance showed.

Without world-class opposition, Gerber's talents would not have been showcased to the world at all, were it not for

the widely condemned New Zealand Cavaliers rebel tour in 1986. Amid outrage from the world press, Kiwis who toured faced being ostracised from their national side. Nevertheless, coached by the legendary Colin Meads, the Cavaliers were still able to bring a very strong side to South Africa. The Springboks were ready and won the tour 3-1, with Gerber putting in some incredible performances, scoring a well-worked try in the third test.

Throughout the international isolation, Gerber was linked with a move to the professional ranks of British rugby league, a move many of his ambitious compatriots were to make. But Gerber had made a promise to Springbok coach Danie Craven that he would refuse all offers, and saw a transition to league as sacrilege.

South Africa were reinstated to international sport in 1992 and Gerber was ready and waiting, scoring two tries in their first test match in their incredibly tight and exhilarating 27-24 loss to New Zealand.

Despite putting in shining performances that seemed to defy his age, at 34, Gerber was nonetheless past his prime. Try-scoring performances against France and a solid performance in his only test against Australia preceded his final test against England at Twickenham, whereupon he called time on his career only five months after his international return.

Just as South Africa were being welcomed back to the international stage, Gerber's time was up. In 1995, three years after his retirement, the Springboks caught the world's imagination by winning the World Cup and they were reluctant to leave their old hero behind. Many Springbok midfielders have tried to emulate Gerber's style and he is fittingly referred to as 'the right man at the wrong time'.

Gerber's career will always be remembered as one tinged

with disappointment for many rugby fans. South Africa's politics deprived the game of one of its most spectacular talents.

While other centres have starred in more famous victories and can boast far more test caps, few captured the imagination in the same way as Danie Gerber. Though many teams will make room for a big and powerful centre, there are none who have had quite the same individual impact on a match. Gerber was built for the more open game, and in the modern era it's unlikely we will ever see a player of his ilk again.

16. J.P.R. WILLIAMS

Full-back, Wales 1969–81

JPR: those three initials are all it takes for Wales fans to be transported back to an era when Wales dominated the world. To be known by one's initials, in a way that still resonates, decades after your retirement indicates the regard in which John Peter Rhys Williams was held, not just by Welsh fans, but by rugby fans the world over.

The distinctive long sideburns, low socks and baggy jersey tearing through the opposition defence, either in the red jersey of Wales or the British & Irish Lions, or the black and white hoops of the Barbarians – JPR's inimitable style made him one of the most instantly recognisable and enduring figures in the history of the sport.

His cavalier approach and disregard for his own safety not only demonstrated his commitment to his team but also

endeared him to a generation of fans. He played as though he were invincible, and indeed he seemed invulnerable to physical punishment, something made all the more surprising when one considers that as an orthopaedic surgeon by trade, JPR was all too familiar with the fragility of the body.

His bravery, coupled with an incredible acceleration as he made his marauding runs, made him a Welsh favourite and one of the most talked-about players that Wales ever produced. What truly made JPR a figure of legend for the Wales fans was his record against the old enemy. In eleven tests against England, JPR was never on the losing side and scored five tries in the process. This outstanding record has never been matched by any of his fellow countrymen. Alongside this impressive record, JPR helped Wales to three grand slams and six triple crowns. He helped ease the hurt felt by English supporters by being a key figure in two of the most iconic British & Irish Lions test series, in 1971 and 1974.

Williams was a courageous player. He was always there when the opposition put the ball high in the air; with astonishing safe hands and an ability to block out any charging defenders, he never seemed to drop the high ball. Once caught, he would storm out of defence with impeccable strength and speed, almost always breaking through his tackle. Complementing this raw athleticism was wonderful handling and a deft touch. All of these skills combined in that 1971 Lions tour in New Zealand when he made a wonder try for Gerald Davies in the second test.

Despite these skills, JPR's selection for the Lions was not a sure thing. There was a raft of talent in the squad, from the likes of England's Bob Hiller and Scotland's Andy Irvine in particular. What JPR lacked next to the other two was ability as a goal-kicker. Williams was well aware of this and it pushed him to improve the other areas of his game, deliberately not working on his goal-kicking, preferring to leave that to others.

Of course, with JPR there was an exception to prove the rule. He only scored one drop-goal in his career, but it was a real beauty. In the fourth and final Lions test in 1971 he landed a 50-yard drop-goal to bring the game level at 14-14, clinching the draw and the Lions' only series win in New Zealand.

Williams played more than a supporting role in several moments in union history. JPR was on the scoresheet in 1973, playing for the Barbarians in their famous victory against the All Blacks. He played his part in what is still remembered as the greatest try ever scored, finished by Gareth Edwards. JPR's own try that day was overshadowed by that brilliance.

He was also an instrumental figure in the implementation of the infamous '99 call' of the 1974 Lions tour (see Willie John McBride, page 130). In the first warm-up game he ran 50 yards just to throw a punch at Boks lock van Heerden as well as throwing a right hook at Tommy Bedford, a moment of history that Williams is not proud of. But the point was made: nobody was going to intimidate a Lions side with JPR on the field.

Another infamous scene came against a touring New Zealand side in 1976, demonstrating JPR's commitment to a competitive cause, as prop forward John Ashworth brutally stamped on his face at a ruck, opening a huge gash on his cheek. As captain, Williams felt that it was his duty to issue instructions to the Bridgend players as he walked from the pitch, blood pouring from the wound. JPR reportedly lost two pints of blood before his father could apply 30 stitches to the wound. He returned to the field and completed the game, which would today be against all medical advice.

Williams was more than just an adrenaline addict though; a complete full-back, he could side-step on the counter-attack and bounce back the juggernaut forwards lucky enough to break the line. Ultimately, his place in history was cemented by virtue of being a part of some of the sweetest moments in the illustrious history of the Wales national side, not least the grand slam victory of 1976. The talented French team of the late 1970s were Wales' main rivals for the Five Nations crown and in a winner-takes-all grand slam final, the Welsh team were narrowly ahead before Jean-François Gourdon broke the line and looked certain to score, until a JPR-shaped red blur swept across the line, smashing him into touch, securing a very special win.

Two years later in 1978, in yet another grand slam final against France (who were champions in 1977), Wales were once again triumphant, a little more comfortably this time. By now the era of JPR, Edwards et al was coming to an end, and it was to be another 27 years before Wales fans would see another grand slam victory.

JPR's international career was cut short prematurely in 1981, not by injury, but by his career as an orthopaedic surgeon. He did, however, continue playing club rugby well into his 50s.

15. PHILIPPE SELLA

Centre, France 1982–95

Just as France were really starting to establish themselves as a force to be reckoned with in world rugby, the first true

Les Bleus stars were emerging. The brightest of these was Philippe Sella. He set the record at the time for the most international caps, with 111, holding down the crucial midfield role for France for well over a decade.

Capable of moments of magic, something he displayed time and time again, Sella had the majestic and highly sought after combination of immense physicality and a deft touch. This made him nearly perfect for any midfield and he takes his place among the most respected and prestigious world-class centres.

An emergent France throughout the 1970s had played with flair and enjoyment, thrilling audiences. Philippe Sella made his debut just after the heroic Jean-Pierre Rives retired, but played alongside Serge Blanco, Franck Mesnel and Pierre Berbizier. It was Sella who was the most exciting of all, charming spectators and tearing apart defences. At his majestic best in 1987, when combining pace and power to enthral and deceive defences across the world, Sella was the lynchpin of a wonderful French back line that on their day would match anybody.

Having played his first few tests on the wing (he made his debut in a shock defeat to Romania in 1982), it wasn't immediate just how much of a special player Les Bleus had. But moving him inside the line to centre brought out the best in his mercurial talent.

It is a shame the world never got to see Philippe Sella against Danie Gerber. Sella was everything that Gerber was not. While they were both world-class centres in the same era, both with the ability to devastate the opposition, Gerber was a very honest rugby player, a straight runner whose mere presence was intimidating. Sella on the other hand was a deceptive runner, someone who popped up in unexpected places. Rather than gathering up speed, he had a sharp

turn of pace and magnificent handling skills. A truly gifted player, Sella excelled in all things subtle and beautiful on the pitch. What's more, in true French fashion, he had a vicious tackle, devastating the opposition ball-carrier whether a wily scrum-half or a giant lock.

As can be expected from someone with an international career spanning thirteen years, Sella formed several fantastic centre partnerships with some incredible players, all with different playing styles that brought out different traits in him. With Didier Codorniou or Denis Charvet outside of him, their straightforward, powerful play allowed Sella the freedom to experiment; with Thierry Lacroix alongside him in the centre line (before Sella retired and Lacroix moved up to fly-half) he was able to provide an incredibly creative midfield with Sella providing some robust defensive back-up.

Sella constantly improved throughout his career and his game matured steadily after his debut, and even more so in the 1986 Five Nations Championship which France shared with Scotland. In this competition Philippe Sella managed a rare feat indeed, scoring a try against every opponent. Sella continued this form into 1987, where he masterminded and controlled the open style France played to win a grand slam in the Five Nations and make it all the way to the World Cup final where they were defeated only by the mighty All Blacks.

Although they were to win the Five Nations Championship three more times with Sella, that was to be his only grand slam. As the years went by, Sella continued to learn and mature and he was still world-class even twelve years into his career, with another memorable moment coming on the French 1994 tour of Canada and New Zealand. The tour did not start well: in true erratic French fashion they entered New Zealand coming off the back of a shock test defeat to Canada, not ideal preparation for the two upcoming test matches against New Zealand, which they were expected to lose heavily. This was not to be the case, with Les Bleus defeating the All Blacks on New Zealand soil in both contests. Although Sella did not score a try himself, he was at his creative best, tearing apart the Kiwi defence in a comfortable 22-8 victory in the first test before displaying his defensive capabilities in the second, a hard-fought 23-20 win against a wounded and fighting All Blacks side.

Philippe Sella ended his international career with a consolation prize in the third-place play-off victory over England in the 1995 World Cup. After a controversial semi-final defeat in the rain to eventual winners South Africa, Sella earned his 111th cap in his final game with an excellent display. France have always performed well in the World Cup and have had their hearts broken in three finals and three semi-finals. They have never looked as likely to win as they did in the time of Serge Blanco and Philippe Sella.

Having played the majority of his club career for French club Agen, Sella took the opportunity to end his career in England, signing his first professional contract with Saracens in 1996. He retired in 1998 having overseen a huge period of transition, not just for France but for the entire world of rugby.

14. SEAN FITZPATRICK

Hooker, New Zealand 1986–97

With hindsight, it seems strange to think that Sean Fitzpatrick's first inclusion into the All Blacks fold was

a hugely fortuitous one, only coming after suspensions and injuries combined to force a huge step up for the inexperienced hooker. This series of events led to the rise to prominence of one of their greatest players ever.

Following the Cavaliers tour of South Africa in 1986, many first-team New Zealand players faced suspensions, leading to the birth of the 'Baby Blacks', the chance for many raw and untested players – potentially the future of the All Blacks – to have a taste of first-class international test rugby.

At the time of his debut, Fitzpatrick only had limited experience at provincial level to draw upon, but with Andy Dalton injured and the second-choice hooker suspended, the chance fell rather unexpectedly for Fitzpatrick, who impressed immediately.

Fortune was once again with Fitzpatrick approaching the 1987 World Cup: just as captain Dalton had worked his way back to fitness, he suffered another injury in training before the first game, leaving Fitzpatrick to play at the centre of the front row for the inaugural World Cup. Despite his novice status, his impact on the squad was not underestimated by the coaches and he was awarded the vice-captaincy.

Between captain and half-back David Kirk leading the side and Fitzpatrick leading the pack, New Zealand were guided to victory, winning every single game of the World Cup by a significant margin. Fitzpatrick was able to immediately step into the boots of the excellent Dalton, who was sadly forced to retire immediately after the World Cup.

Fitzpatrick's emergence coincided with an almost unbeatable national side. The squad was full of stars, many of whom were the best in the world in their positions and who collectively were almost unstoppable. And although Fitzpatrick was still only approaching his prime, by the time the 1991 World Cup rolled around, many of these stars were past their best and were perhaps complacent about their ability to beat their rivals. There was a steep learning curve as they were humiliated by Australia, the Wallabies recording a 21-12 semi-final victory over the tournament favourites, leading to the retirement of many All Blacks icons.

A coaching revolution followed, with Laurie Mains installing Fitzpatrick as captain in 1992. Fitzpatrick was kept on his toes throughout the '90s by an intense rivalry with Australian Phil Kearns, which drew the best rugby from both hookers (despite some questionable sledging and sportsmanship along the way). Kearns was a very physical player whose strength matched up to Fitzpatrick's technical approach. Over the years they were well matched, with both men enjoying successes and failures in the Bledisloe Cup and other test series.

Fitzpatrick was able to cope with all the physical demands of test rugby in the front row, but his motivational abilities as a leader and his immense mental strength are what elevate him over his peers into the upper echelons of rugby history. The New Zealand side at the time were admired for their resilient and solid pack and Fitzpatrick stood out as the star.

The toughest mental test that Sean Fitzpatrick faced in those years of captaincy came with the visit of the British & Irish Lions in 1993. The Lions side arrived, captained by Gavin Hastings, who had a wonderful tour as he led the combination of stars from the home nations to a second test victory, leading to a series decider in Auckland and the possibility of Fitzpatrick being only the second captain to allow a series defeat by the Lions. The team rallied behind their captain, however, and a comprehensive 30-13 victory in the final test reasserted New Zealand's dominance.

New Zealand made a barnstorming entrance to the 1995 World Cup, with Jonah Lomu stealing all the headlines, but disappointment followed after many of the squad were struck down with food poisoning on the night before the final against bitter rivals South Africa. Francois Pienaar and his Springboks stunned the favourites and an extra-time drop-goal from Joel Stransky broke New Zealand hearts once again and Fitzpatrick returned home empty-handed.

Following this disappointment, Fitzpatrick and the All Blacks entered the world of professional rugby as the most disciplined and well-drilled side in the world. Training even harder than before to redeem themselves from another heartbreaking World Cup defeat, Fitzpatrick led New Zealand to their first ever series win on South African soil the next year. A hard-fought series win required Fitzpatrick at his most stubborn, with New Zealand not able to rely on their skill alone to defeat the world champions; they played with immense heart, with their captain leading by example.

A tour of Europe followed in 1997, which saw a decline in Fitzpatrick's physical fitness. A chronic knee injury limited his mobility on the pitch and although New Zealand were still winning tests with Fitzpatrick at the heart of the scrum, he was playing through the pain and retired before this affected results.

13. GEORGE SMITH

Flanker, Australia 2000–13

Alongside Richie McCaw, George Smith stands out as the greatest openside flanker of his generation. From his debut against France in 2000 to what was likely his final game for

Australia against the Lions in 2013, Smith was consistently world class, maintaining his form and playing a huge role in every success the Wallabies enjoyed for an astonishing thirteen years. He is the second-most capped flanker in international test history, with 111 test matches played.

Making both his professional and international debuts in the year 2000, aged twenty, Smith's work rate and skill at the breakdown was invaluable to Australia. His rise to fame was meteoric, and his ability to turn the ball was a trait he would quickly become known for as he strengthened his reputation as one of the sport's leading players.

It didn't take long for Smith's potential to be realised, as a man-of-the-match performance in the deciding test against the British & Irish Lions on his 21st birthday proved. A hero of the tour, he proved himself to be a more than competent and highly intelligent ball-carrier, a truly lethal openside. Smith had appeared in all three tests of the tour and they were the highest-profile games he had yet played in. In the first test, the Lions presented a new challenge as Smith lined up against the vastly more experienced Neil Back and Richard Hill as his opposition back row. That wasn't all: the Lions brought huge support with them, and the stadium was a sea of red, meaning Australia's home advantage counted for nothing. This Lions team had some all-time greats; alongside Brian O'Driscoll, Keith Wood and Martin Johnson was the union introduction of Jason Robinson (who scored a wonderful try). The Lions won this first test and Australia, the world champions, had been outplayed. It was a shock to the system for Smith, but he was able to keep his composure thanks to the dressing-room experience the Wallabies had in their squad, players like John Eales and George Gregan. Smith's response in that final test lives on in Wallabies legend.

His excellent form continued into the domestic season and in 2002 a superb campaign with the Brumbies saw him awarded the inaugural John Eales Medal, which is given by the Australian Rugby Union Players Association to their player of the year.

Smith was perfect at all of the things that a back row needs to be perfect at. With nobody as technically brilliant in the breakdown, there were matches where Smith's turnover rate could match the entire opposition team. Although he started his career as a ground hog, a tackle poacher, like many flankers, he improved with age, as he added more skills to his game. He was always a rock in defence, but he was ferocious enough to recover, stand and immediately bridge over to win a penalty for his side or turn the ball over. This requires tremendous core strength, to be able to squat and bridge over the ball without going to ground, even with the opposition smashing into him. Strength and bravery were key factors in Smith's achievements.

He stepped up his game against the most elite opponents. He has faced up against some of the best outside halves ever in the shape of Dan Carter and Jonny Wilkinson and he made them well aware of his presence. Although the work of a flanker doesn't always steal the headlines or capture the imagination of the crowd, Smith has drawn audible sympathetic grunts from spectators as he's smashed into fly-halves like Carter. His work has been instrumental in bringing rare success for Australia against their neighbouring arch-rivals. And although Australia have lost more Bledisloe Cups than they have won in recent years, suggesting that overall Carter has won this particular battle, Smith has shown often enough that he has the ability to shut a fly-half down, and can single-handedly cripple the opposition. Smith is a textbook tackler, he would dive and squeeze the legs of a breaking centre in a cover tackle, or send a tight charging forward backwards. When he was paired with the excellent scrum-half Gregan, Australia were masters of fast recycling. It was a strong feature of any back row containing Smith that they would smash into a ruck and were drilled to the point where Gregan was able to use the ball quickly and they were able to maintain several phases of play at breakneck speed, a feature of play that was particularly devastating for northern hemisphere teams at the time.

With all of the attention on his support play and his defensive capabilities, Smith's attacking prowess was often overlooked. And while it's true that he was not the greatest at simply smashing his way over the gain line, he was still a prolific attacking player, particularly in the latter part of his career. Rather than simply break through, again it was a superior technique that allowed for this. A great handoff of the mighty Brian O'Driscoll in the 2013 Lions tour displayed this area of his game excellently. Smith was also able to kick and chase proficiently and on occasion was even known to put his boot on to a grubber. A brave player, Smith had an excellent eye for the try line, making chargedowns and completing the kind of offloads that a top rugby league player would envy.

Smith took part in two World Cup campaigns for Australia, and although the 2007 campaign was a disappointment, he played in all seven games of the 2003 World Cup where the Wallabies reached the final, including a famous victory against New Zealand in the semi-final. Despite this long and illustrious career, Smith only won two Bledisloe Cups in the ten that he competed in and was only ever involved in one Tri-Nations victory.

George Smith announced his retirement from inter-national rugby in 2010, ten years after making his debut against France, surprising many by going to play at club level in the emerging rugby nation of Japan.

Almost as surprising as his departure was his shock return to the Brumbies in 2013, whereupon he made himself available for international selection again and once again took a crucial role in an Australian test series victory over a touring British & Irish Lions side.

Smith then made himself ineligible for international selection once more with a move to France to play his club rugby with Stade Français and Lyon. With Lyon in particular, he displayed excellent form and there was even talk of an international comeback when the eligibility rules for overseas players changed; he was placed as back-up to some incredible young Wallabies back-row players but with Australia having the luxury of a host of world-class openside flankers in the likes of Michael Hooper and the sublime David Pocock, Smith was left out of the squad for the 2015 World Cup. As Smith ages and shows no sign of slowing down, one can still dream that he might yet earn a recall to the Wallabies squad.

12. JOOST VAN DER WESTHUIZEN

Scrum-half, South Africa 1993–2003

The greatest scrum-half of the modern era, Joost van der Westhuizen was capped a total of 89 times during a ten-year international career and was a crucial member of the Springboks side that lifted the 1995 Rugby World Cup.

Now, when talking about that side, it's important to acknowledge the impact of Francois Pienaar. He was an incredible leader and a great player; but in pure rugby terms Joost van der Westhuizen was the one player South Africa could not have won the World Cup without.

As well as an inspirational story, the South Africa World Cup victory of 1995 is arguably the most influential in the history of the sport. South Africa had only just returned to the international stage and for them to win on home soil, with the world watching, had huge ramifications for the development of the rugby world. Accusations of food poisoning and disallowed French tries aside, the political and social ramifications of South Africa's victory are well documented, as was Pienaar's crucial role in that victory. But there was also some rugby played, and it is astonishing that the major motion picture *Invictus* manages to entirely ignore the Springboks' star scrum-half.

Fearless in defence as well as a shrewd try scorer, 'the sniper', as he was often known, had an uncanny ability to read a game and think several phases of play ahead. The South African rugby team is known for pace and for power as well as unrivalled technical prowess, and when Joost van der Westhuizen announced his – and South Africa's – arrival on the international scene, he was soon lauded as the greatest player in the world. Joost controlled every game from the breakdown with what can only be described as rugby genius.

At the dawn of professionalism, and of a new nation, the pressure was incredible on the 24-year-old. With an 'underdogs' tag and a point to prove, the preparation for the World Cup involved hard training, tough physical sessions and intense conditioning. This physical presence has been a cornerstone of every South African team since. Van der Westhuizen was no exception. He suffered a broken rib in the semi-final and played every minute of the final only a week later after seven painkilling injections.

Two of the three most iconic moments of the final (beaten only by the sight of Nelson Mandela in a Springbok shirt) belong to Joost. The element of surprise that South Africa enjoyed after their international exile meant that no side quite knew how to play them, but the real surprise package of that World Cup was Jonah Lomu. Lomu had almost single-handedly destroyed the English in the quarter-final and yet could not find his way past this Bokke scrum-half. Time and time again the giant Kiwi had powered up and not once did he get past the number nine. There was one instance in particular when Lomu was up to full pace and did manage to find his way through the South African midfield until van der Westhuizen – with a broken rib and as the smallest man on the pitch – recovered and stopped a certain try with a textbook tackle on the beast.

The other defining moment for van der Westhuizen in the final was his involvement in the winning drop-goal. Joel Stransky may have scored the points, but the reason why he had so much time was down to van der Westhuizen. The New Zealand scrum-half Graeme Bachop decided to mark his opposite number at the foot of the scrum instead of lining up against the number ten. This was a risky move, as Bachop knew that the ball was going to Stransky, but by concentrating on van der Westhuizen, the pressure was now on the Bokke who had only a split-second to move the ball along. Joost reacted and cancelled the planned move and gambled that he'd have enough time to get the ball away. Bachop was unable to stop the pass, due to the quick hands and skill of Joost. This left Stransky now completely unmarked, with all the time he needed to comfortably slot the ball home for the World Cup.

Throughout the competition and the external pressure that was on this Springbok side, the young van der

Westhuizen remained calm. A true competitor, he said, 'We are sportsmen, we just want to play rugby, we are not politicians'. That may be true, but his skill on the rugby pitch had an incredible impact on the politics of the rainbow nation.

His outstanding service to the Springboks did not end in 1995. Joost van der Westhuizen participated in a total of three Rugby World Cups and he was given the honour of leading his country in an attempt to retain the Webb Ellis trophy in 1999. Once again, the scrum-half was a key player and South Africa only lost after a long and hard-fought semi-final against eventual winners Australia, being knocked out by a last-minute Stephen Larkham drop-goal.

He was a big guy for a scrum-half and a real competitive animal. But as scoring goes, the no-nonsense number nine also crossed for a record 38 test tries in his career – which remains the highest number of test tries a scrum-half has scored, by some distance. In fact, the only Springbok to have scored more is the legendary Bryan Habana. As an all-round footballer, it's hard to find a better inclusion into a dream team than Joost van der Westhuizen.

11. JOHN EALES

Lock, Australia 1991–2001

Nicknamed 'Nobody', because 'nobody's perfect', John Eales possessed pretty much every single skill the modern rugby player requires. He was mobile, had fantastic handling skills and was rarely beaten at the lineout. He had an immense ability to read the game, didn't shy from a tackle, had a huge work rate – oh, and he was a lock who could kick for goal. All of these qualities, combined with his inspirational leadership and incredible sportsmanship, make this nickname well earned.

A career total of 173 points for a forward is enormous and the sight of the big second-row lining up kicks at goal always beggared belief, but he was a highly successful goal-kicker, and it's tough to argue with the statistics, which include several high-profile match-winning penalties under immense pressure.

The most successful captain in the history of Australian rugby, and the highest-scoring forward ever in test rugby, Eales' career began in trademark spotless fashion. Eales earned his first international honours in 1991, in a 63-6 victory over Wales. From there, it was on to England for the second ever Rugby World Cup and, aged 21, in only his second game, he managed to dominate established England lock Martin Bayfield as the Aussies steamrollered an England side straight off the back of a Five Nations grand slam victory. His arrival immediately got critics excited and expectations mounted, with the media, fans and coaches all certain that they were watching somebody a bit special.

Australia seemed to be in somewhat of a rut after their 1991 World Cup victory. Several fruitless years went by without them winning a Tri-Nations tournament (the young Eales still put in some excellent performances), but they started to turn around their fortunes upon the arrival of coach Rod Macqueen in 1997, just as Eales came of age.

Much of Australia's success in the late 1990s and early 2000s hinged on this successful partnership between Eales and Macqueen. Australia's capture of the World Cup in 1999 was built on outstanding defence and clinical rugby football, brilliantly planned and executed by coach Rod Macqueen and his captain Eales. With this success Eales became one of just a handful of players to have won the World Cup twice.

The clearest indications of Australia's success, outside of the 1999 World Cup win, were their retention of the Bledisloe Cup over arch-rivals New Zealand between 1998 and 2002, and the two Tri-Nations titles of 2000 and 2001. Indeed, those two Tri-Nations wins under Eales remain Australia's only successes in that tournament. And to win five successive Bledisloe Cups, when previously they had only ever managed to win two on the bounce in the history of the competition, is staggering.

Accompanying his clear technical ability, Eales was thoroughly accomplished as a captain, tactically astute and a charismatic leader. In many ways Eales was similar to the future Martin Johnson – but in others the polar opposite. Like Johnson he was a strong and dependable lock who took the responsibility of the team on his shoulders, allowing his players the freedom to express themselves. Unlike Johnson, however, Eales was almost universally liked by neutrals and his enjoyment for the game was felt by spectators and players alike.

Like many of the true greats, Eales decided to end his international career while at the peak of his game. One of his last challenges came in the shape of Martin Johnson's British & Irish Lions. After losing the first test, the Wallabies went on to win the series 2-1, becoming the first Australian team in history to defeat the Lions.

Fittingly, Eales' final game was a Bledisloe Cup match in Sydney against the All Blacks. In a period of classic tussles between these two giants of world rugby, this match was another dramatic encounter. With Australia leading comfortably, New Zealand stormed back to take the lead in

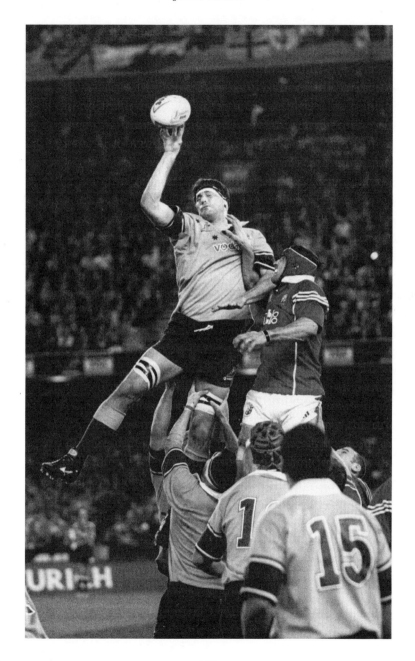

the closing stages, setting up a dramatic finale before the Wallabies scored a last-gasp try to win the game and Eales was able to sign off in style. He ended his international career in 2001 with 86 caps and having won every trophy available in the sport.

Along with an impressive international record, Eales enjoyed great domestic success as well. Playing his domestic rugby for the Queensland Reds, he remains the all-time points scorer for a forward in the Super 12 competition. It is indicative of the esteem in which he is held in Australia – where they have their fair share of rugby greats – that since 2002 the John Eales Medal has been awarded annually to the best Australian rugby union player.

10. ZINZAN BROOKE

Number eight, New Zealand 1987–97

Built like a tree but with the handling ability of a back line star, Zinzan Brooke was one of the first prolific modern number eights, and one of the best all-round players ever to set foot on a rugby pitch.

Unconventional in every sense, Brooke combined brute strength and agility in the breakdown with a deft touch and a strong kicking game. He was an utterly brilliant and unique player who revolutionised what was expected of a number eight. He was a rock at the heart of the New Zealand defence throughout the 1990s, but his contributions included a number of important drop-goals that any fly-half would have been delighted with.

His unorthodox style meant that he was not an automatic selection for the All Blacks for many years, despite impressing and scoring a try on his debut against Argentina in the 1987 World Cup. Zinzan had to settle for a back-up place to Wayne 'Buck' Shelford and only really got a chance when he was injured – and even then there were times when Zinzan wasn't selected, with Michael Jones sometimes shifted around the back line instead. Only when Shelford was dropped aged 33 did Brooke get his chance for a regular run in the All Blacks first team.

This was a transitional period for New Zealand: many of the players taken to the 1991 World Cup were perhaps past their best and after their semi-final defeat against the Wallabies, all the players were tarred with the same brush, so that even the younger ones were perceived as failures.

One bright spark to retain his reputation following the World Cup failure was the talismanic captain, hooker Sean Fitzpatrick. Fitzpatrick was a fierce supporter of Brooke and managed to convince the new All Blacks coach Laurie Mains that the number eight was worthy of selection and a chance for redemption on their upcoming tour of Australia and a one-off test in South Africa. Mains was sceptical of Brooke's unusual approach and believed that his work ethic in close international tests would not hold up to scrutiny, and that his style would come to the detriment of the rest of the side.

But Brooke was selected on that tour and he rewarded his coach's gamble and his captain's faith with unrelenting ferocity and controlled aggression in all of the traditional areas that his coach needed while still maintaining the canny invention that made Brooke so exceptional. Victories against a touring Lions side in 1993 and South African side in 1994 led to Brooke becoming a key member of Mains' squad.

In their build-up to the World Cup in 1995, Brooke damaged his Achilles tendon, which was a major blow. After receiving specialist treatment and playing with several painkilling injections, Brooke had an astonishing tournament, being the standout loose forward for New Zealand as they and Jonah Lomu smashed their way through their opposition until they met England in the semi-final. There the All Blacks were at their best as they amassed a huge 45 points, three of those coming from an audacious drop-goal from the storming number eight, Zinzan Brooke. A forward scoring a drop-goal of any description is always worthy of note but this one, coming in the semi-final, while on the run, from the touchline, only just inside the opposition half, was nothing short of astonishing and goes down as one of the finest moments of World Cup history. Brooke's joy was to be short-lived, however, as the All Blacks were defeated by the host nation South Africa in the historic final. The heartbreak and indignation of the defeat did not sit well with Brooke or his teammates. They still believed they were the best team on the planet.

The response from the All Blacks was tremendous. There followed two seasons of magnificence, culminating in New Zealand's only ever series victory over South Africa away from their home soil. Brooke scored two tries on that tour and in the test that clinched the series scored yet another magnificent drop-goal, proving once again on the highest stage that his talent was no fluke. Brooke's career was coming to a close, however, and he and his captain Fitzpatrick were to play their final games in the autumn of '97. There was still time for Brooke to showcase his cavalier approach and drop another goal against Wales in a test match at Wembley in his penultimate (and Fitzpatrick's final) test. New Zealand won 42-7.

What began as an unorthodox approach led to other number eights across the world having to adapt and improve their game to match. With Brooke scoring seventeen test tries in his career, he paved the way the much more attacking-minded number eight and for players like Colin Charvis for Wales, Lawrence Dallaglio for England and now even Kieran Read for New Zealand. The number eight of today is expected to be so much more than the base of a scrum; an all-round number eight is crucial to the balance of the team, and much of this approach is down to the effectiveness of the likes of Zinzan Brooke.

Following his heroics against Wales, Brooke's final test came in a draw against England at Twickenham in 1997. After retiring from international rugby, Brooke moved to England and played for the Harlequins until he retired in 2001, aged 36.

9. JONNY WILKINSON

Fly-half, England 1998–2011

Jonny Wilkinson will forever be remembered as the man who kicked England to Rugby World Cup victory in 2003 – a last-gasp drop-goal in extra-time to defeat the hosts made for the most dramatic of tournament finales. What was even more remarkable was that iconic drop-goal, the moment that cemented his place in English sporting history, was scored with his less favoured right boot.

But that is just one highlight from a record-breaking career that made Wilkinson one of the sport's all-time greats. If there's any justice, that kick is not where the story ends, and while it's fair to say that he dragged England to many a charmless victory by his very own bootlaces, this was a player who had far more to offer than just his goal kicks.

But it's impossible to talk about Wilkinson without talking about his kicking ability. To kick goals to that standard – more drop-goals than any other international player ever – doesn't just happen overnight. To say that Wilko took training seriously is an understatement, he was obsessive and there's no doubt at all that he was a perfectionist. He has often described his love of training, how it was the only time he was able to relax. He has talked of his fear on match days, and while this is not unique, it's important to attempt to acknowledge the complex psyche of Jonny Wilkinson as his was a career that trod the line between mental strength and an incredible work ethic. After he was under intense scrutiny following a perceived drop in form after a plague of injuries, this ability to perform under pressure was vital, enabling him to return to such impressive form that he was named European Player of the Year in the twilight of his career.

In the run-up to the 2003 World Cup, when England enjoyed a fit and injury-free Jonny Wilkinson, the tactics seemed to be to simply keep play in the right area of the field, wait for the penalty or drop-goal opportunity and allow the points to accrue. All it took was a slight lapse in discipline or concentration and Wilkinson could quickly take the game away from you. In these times, England's play was not always a thing of beauty: there were games where Jonny scored every single one of England's points, such as the semi-final of the 2003 World Cup against France in the pouring rain.

But for all of his kicking ability, Wilkinson hit like a back-rower. It's testament to the man's stubborn nature that he wasn't content with simply tackling a player, but anyone that came into his channel was sent backwards. Regardless of size, and regardless of the speed or momentum of the attacking player, he would stop them dead. He undoubtedly paid the price with the physical damage inflicted on his own body. Even late into his career, after all of the injuries, he still led with his shoulder and was the cause of much exhaling from commentators and fans, as well as the shattering effect on the opposition player.

For a time, Wilkinson was one of the most recognisable faces in any sport. The 2003 IRB Player of the Year and BBC Sports Personality of the Year, Wilkinson also had a constant sponsorship presence with countless companies fighting to be associated with the exciting (and, importantly, teetotal and squeaky clean) England role model. During this time Wilkinson endorsed many products, provided weekly newspaper columns and published several books and DVDs while still managing to retain an air of genuine humility – quite a feat.

Yet, at the first sign of poor form, he was torn apart by the press and it noticeably affected his game. There was an inexorable link between the things that made Jonny a great role model (and player), and the insecurities that plagued a large section of his career. He would obsess over how the press represented him, took every criticism personally. His teammates, who were impressed by his work rate and professionalism, were sometimes worried about the effect that his excessive training and extreme attitude to training were having on his mental health.

His international career was traumatic and turbulent from the start. A young Wilkinson was a member of the 'Tour of Hell' in 1998 that saw huge defeats at the hands of Australia (the first match was a hefty 76-0), New Zealand and

South Africa. But it proved to be a learning experience for Wilkinson, who was the bright spark of a resurgent England who went from strength to strength in the years leading up to the World Cup in Australia.

Following that night in Sydney in 2003, Wilkinson's career was blighted by injury. Knee ligament, arm, shoulder and kidney problems meant he did not appear again for England for more than three years. In fact, he was determined to be ready for the next World Cup and first appeared in England's opening game of the 2007 Six Nations Championship. In his comeback England match, Wilkinson scored a Calcutta Cup record of 27 points in a man-of-the-match performance. The following week, against Italy, he became the highest points scorer in the history of the Five/Six Nations Championship.

Injury problems returned later that season and it became clear that these physical injuries only told half of the story; the mental suffering that went along with it arguably had a bigger long-term effect on his game. Despite this, Jonny battled back to be part of England's World Cup squad who surprised many by making their way to the final, only to lose to South Africa.

With his injury record, England could not rely on Wilkinson to be the centre of their game plan. His position when fit was no longer guaranteed as England experimented with new tactics and a new generation of stars targeting the fly-half position. Wilkinson was dropped and Danny Cipriani was preferred for the final match of the 2008 Six Nations Championship against Ireland. Wilkinson was then left out of England's summer tour to New Zealand and underwent yet more shoulder surgery at the end of the season.

England could not find a successor that could settle: Cipriani's off-the-field antics ruled him out, and Hodgson, Barkley, Goode et al were either uninspiring or unreliable

– at least, when compared to Wilkinson. England always seemed to play with one eye on the injury table, but yet more knee and shoulder injuries kept Wilkinson away for another two years, before he returned for the 2010 Six Nations, and a stuttering return to form began before the 2011 World Cup.

During a disappointing World Cup for England, Wilkinson started four of England's five games, including the quarter-final against France. His performances didn't seem to match up to those earlier in his career – his kicking statistics were no longer as impressive – leading to question marks over his selection, although much of the criticism was once again from the press.

Despite all of the absences due to injury he managed a staggering 91 caps and remains, to date, England's second-most capped player of all time behind Jason Leonard. One could speculate as to whether he reached this remarkable tally in part by often rushing back from injury and playing when not up to his best. But it is also true that England were a better team with Wilkinson playing. With Wilkinson in the team, England won 67 games out of a possible 91, a win rate that is difficult to ignore.

Wilkinson announced his international retirement following the 2011 World Cup. A new English RFU policy meant that he was ineligible for selection as he played his club rugby outside of the country. But as many in England considered Wilkinson to be past his best, he continued to shine for Toulon and in 2013 was named European Player of the Year as Toulon won the Heineken Cup. Wilkinson went through the knockout stages of the competition without missing a single kick – an incredible seventeen penalties in a row, plus two drop-goals – leading many to question England's selection policy and call for his return. Sadly, this was not to be.

Even despite the less than consistent form and injury plight, Wilkinson has to be considered not only one of England rugby's greatest ever players, but one of the greatest players ever to play the game. What's more remarkable is that he would probably disagree with that statement. One has to take into account his impact both on and off the pitch. After that World Cup win, the amount of kids showing up to play mini rugby, right the way through to Colts, was staggering. Stuart Lancaster said that the latest generation of players are all trying to emulate Jonny's professional attitude to training, his willingness to learn, as well as his technical ability. It may be controversial to say that on his day Wilkinson was the greatest fly-half ever to play the game (a certain Kiwi would contest this), but what cannot be disputed is that with one drop-goal, Wilkinson changed the profile and esteem in which English rugby was held by the general public.

8. JONAH LOMU

Wing, New Zealand 1994–2002

For millions of sport fans throughout the world, Jonah Lomu will forever be remembered as the personification of power. He was a superstar that utterly transcended rugby, inspiring thousands of new fans in the process, introducing them to a new sport with some of the greatest individual performances the game has ever seen.

As the very first global rugby superstar, Lomu's very presence accelerated the development of professionalism to the game we know today. Those who were fortunate enough to witness Jonah Lomu ignite the 1995 World Cup by laying defences to waste will never forget the impact he had on the unsuspecting home nations. Weighing in at over eighteen stone, and able to run the 100 metres in under eleven seconds, he was a physical phenomenon with the ability to simply run over a potential tackler, or as Will Carling kindly put it, Lomu was 'a freak'.

The name Jonah Lomu resonates with a whole generation of rugby supporters. For those who were introduced to the sport around this time, he gave a first glimpse of the raw entertainment it could provide. In the highest-profile World Cup to date, youngsters watching couldn't help but be fascinated by someone with such an obvious impact. Arguably the single most iconic man in rugby's history, in the '90s, his name was synonymous with the sport. The marketing was intensive: he had computer games named after him – in fact there was little point sponsoring any other superstar at the time. Lomu was the man who was worth everything.

But let's focus on the rugby. It had been a twisting, uncertain path to tournament selection for Lomu in 1995 and while he made the cut, he only really had experience playing Sevens for the All Blacks. However, while playing second row for Counties Manukau, they needed someone to cover out on the wing. In front of the selectors he scored four tries out there and was brought into the squad for his international debut against France in June 1994. Although he didn't score and his performance was far from polished, the coaches saw the potential there and selected him for the World Cup.

Ireland had no idea what they were up against when they faced New Zealand in their first group game. They were already underdogs and were coming to terms with the prospect of lining up against the likes of Frank Bunce, Sean

Fitzpatrick and Zinzan Brooke, among others. They hadn't factored anyone like Jonah Lomu into their game plan – how could they have? It took about twenty minutes for Lomu to get his first touch, but as soon as he did Ireland were in tatters. Two first-half tries laid the Irish to waste; they were unable to recover or muster a reply to a man they simply could not tackle. Ireland put up a fight and played an offensive game of their own, but ultimately the difference was Lomu and the steady boot of the All Blacks fly-half Andrew Mehrtens as they finished the game 43-19 with, crucially, five tries to Ireland's three.

Lomu made a similar impact against Wales in their next group game, despite not scoring himself, as the All Blacks won comfortably. Scotland tried to prepare themselves for the quarter-final and much of the pre-match talk in the press was dominated by how they would stop Lomu, with Gavin Hastings stating that it was an impossible task, and that proved to be no joke.

His greatest performance, and arguably the best individual performance from any player in a World Cup, came against England in the semi-final. It only took two minutes for Lomu's impact to be felt and for him to score his first try, brushing aside a hopeful England, who had fancied themselves as finalists, bringing the nation crashing down to earth. Lomu went on to score four tries in this historic encounter, the most famous of which being when he brushed off Will Carling, and the enduring image of full-back Mike Catt being tipped on his back in a crushing and comical fashion as Lomu ran literally straight over him, humiliating one of England's greatest ever players, before diving over the try line. The game finished 45-29 and ineffectual England were left shell-shocked and bewildered.

Nobody had ever seen a player like Lomu before and

rivals Australia had managed to get through the 1995 World Cup without facing the juggernaut force. That was not to last for long as they faced each other a month later in Sydney and Lomu displayed all of the same qualities to score one try and make another three as New Zealand won 34-23. Without Lomu, New Zealand would not have been anywhere near the side they were. Although they were full of quality players, other nations were catching up. But with Jonah in the side, nobody was able to shut them out. His acceleration was phenomenal and with such agility, balance and brute strength, no defender could get near him. It was an absolute masterstroke to put Lomu out on the wing. He had no right to be as quick as he was, but with all of the other aspects he brought to the game, he changed what was to be expected from a wide man forever. Teams weren't able to simply place a nippy guy out wide and tell him to wait for the ball. A defender facing Lomu stood little chance; he was an astonishing athlete.

Completely unknown to the entire world, and although he had been feeling the effects for some time, Lomu was diagnosed with a serious and rare kidney disorder in 1996. Lomu had played in the '95 World Cup knowing that he was sick; his body felt the effects of every game, with the symptoms of his condition including severe tiredness, making Lomu's achievements all the more remarkable. Nobody watching his dramatic play would have twigged just how unwell Lomu was – not least Mike Catt. Following the diagnosis, Lomu took some time away from the sport and did not play in the 1997 World Rugby Championship. It must be said, though, that while health issues were having an effect on his game and his physical well-being, he was still able to force sides to re-evaluate their entire tactics, and coaches to hastily arrange plans to desperately try to shut Lomu out of the game.

Even with continuing problems, Lomu displayed phenomenal mental strength to match his extraordinary physical
might, and reached the pinnacle of his game once more to
make selection for the 1999 World Cup, participating again
in the competition which he so completely personifies.

In the 1999 World Cup, even with Lomu's condition and
the changes that professionalism had made to the physique
and fitness of the players – not to mention opponents having
four years to prepare for him – Lomu managed to score even
more tries than in '95. Even without the element of surprise,
Lomu was just as devastating, scoring a record-breaking
eight tries in the tournament, once again laying England
and Scotland to waste before scoring two first-half tries in
the semi-final against France, leaving stunned defenders
scattered in his wake.

Ultimately, France were able to complete one of the
greatest comebacks in the history of the sport to win the
game 43-31 in a thrilling encounter. With the New Zealand
side devastated, Lomu remained on the pitch to congratulate
the winning side and applaud the travelling fans, a display of
grace from the gentle giant.

As Lomu's health deteriorated he continued to be a
wonderful and dedicated ambassador for the sport. Instead
of demanding superstar treatment, he moved to play briefly
for Second Division Wainuiomata RFC, drawing in record
crowds and distributing the new-found popularity for the
sport through the tiers. That's not to say that Lomu was not
able to produce world-class displays, but they came only
sporadically. Arguably one of his finest moments came in
what many consider the greatest game of rugby ever played
between Australia and New Zealand, in the 2000 Bledisloe
Cup encounter. With Tana Umaga scoring a try within two
minutes to set the tone for this furious encounter, Lomu

powered down the touchline to set up a second try, and remarkably a third followed, all within the first five minutes. Australia, led by the great John Eales, did not lie down and astonishingly managed to score three tries themselves to make the scores level by half-time. The second half continued in this fashion and Australia found themselves ahead 35-34 approaching injury time, before Lomu finished off a well-worked move to win the game 39-35.

Following Jonah Lomu's entrance and the World Cup of 1995, greater emphasis was placed on the physical aspect of the game. Desperate not to repeat the humiliation, northern hemisphere sides in particular became obsessed with size, speed and strength, perhaps to the detriment of natural skill and instinct. The money, sponsorship, and reams of new fans that Lomu is associated with brought added pressure and changed the game of rugby forever.

Lomu is potentially the individual who had the single greatest impact on the game. He was the embodiment of the World Cup for many and he continued to work with, represent and promote the competition until his untimely death following the 2015 tournament. There was never a player quite like Lomu before he arrived; many have since tried to emulate him, but none has ever quite had the impact.

7. DAN CARTER

Fly-half, New Zealand 2003–15

As the poster boy for world rugby's most successful side ever, the expectations and pressures that Dan Carter faced matched up to his mercurial talents. New Zealand had enjoyed a heroic outside half since the inaugural World Cup and before, with Grant Fox through to Andrew Mehrtens guiding the All Blacks to success, but they have all been eclipsed by Dan Carter. More than just an unstoppable point-scoring machine (and the record holder for most international points scored), Carter was one of the most complete players ever to play the game.

He made his debut at inside centre against Wales in 2003, scoring a try and impressing enough to be included in their World Cup squad later that year. Putting in accomplished performances, again from midfield, in group games against Tonga and Italy, in the more important games he came from the bench as a bit-part player, replacing Carlos Spencer against South Africa and France. He didn't feature at all in New Zealand's defeat to Australia, with Carlos Spencer playing the full 80 minutes. But it would not take long for Carter to usurp Spencer as New Zealand's first-choice number ten. As wonderful a player as Spencer was – he was reliable and his boot brought New Zealand many victories – world-class opposition could forecast his movements and he lacked that extra bit of creativity that Carter would eventually bring. Anybody who predicted at that time that Carter would use precisely these abilities to be the future of New Zealand rugby would have been bursting with pride at his performance in the final twelve years later.

The drop-goal he scored that day signified exactly what made Carter stand head and shoulders above his opposition. With Australia fighting back and clawing their way back into the game, taking advantage of the All Blacks having a man in the sin bin to reduce the deficit to four points, Carter stepped up to score a sensational and crucial three points. He gave the Wallabies no chance to read the play; without sitting deep in the pocket to buy himself time and space, he had to take the ball and score in one movement. It was an audacious moment, one which once again took the game out of Australia's reach and a pivotal moment in the final, one which his opponents could only admire – stunned and defeated.

The first occasion where Carter's ability left spectators breathless was in 2005, against the British & Irish Lions. In a complete fly-half performance, Carter scored a staggering 33 points during the 48-18 annihilation, including two storming tries. This catapulted him to a new audience and higher expectations, but after a stand-out year that also included victory in the Tri-Nations, Carter was named IRB Player of the Year.

The only small blemish on Carter's career is a significant one, playing his part in the All Blacks' worst-ever World Cup in 2007, crashing out in the quarter-finals against the most unpredictable of hosts, Les Bleus. It was a rare defeat for New Zealand and one which showed that even the greatest of teams are capable of a momentary mental lapse on the greatest stage. They quickly recovered and Carter was on top form in New Zealand's Tri-Nations success the following year.

Further World Cup heartbreak followed in 2011. After positive performances in the group games, Carter tore a tendon in his groin the day before the match against Canada. The tragedy of losing a great player in his prime on the greatest stage was felt, but the All Blacks became champions without him, with Stephen Donald filling in at fly-half. The criticism that Donald faced on the way to the final, where he ultimately kicked the winning penalty, shows the incredibly high expectations that come with wearing the All Blacks jersey.

There were some who did not expect Carter to be quite the same player if and when he returned, but those doubters were proven wrong when he returned in time for the 2012 Rugby Championship and was immediately on top form, helping the All Blacks secure an unbeaten competition. He was rewarded with his second IRB Player of the Year award, joining his captain Richie McCaw as the only other player to win the award more than once.

With his eyes on the retention of the World Cup, one that would likely be his last, Carter focused on remaining fit and in form for 2015. He never shied away from contact and kept putting his body on the line at fly-half, his style of play bringing him face-to-face with some back-row forwards whose sole aim was to bully Carter off the pitch and the result was a string of injuries. At the start of 2014, Carter took a break from rugby for several months. Although he only missed a handful of All Blacks test matches, he took the time to rest his body, iron out a few injuries and push his body with an intense fitness regime. In the meantime, the youthful Beauden Barrett was ready to step into the number 10 jersey. Dan Carter had to work hard to reclaim his position in the starting line-up, but as the World Cup approached, there was only ever going to be one All Blacks fly-half.

And so, just as England relied on Wilkinson in 2003, South Africa on Habana in 2007, and New Zealand on McCaw in 2011, 2015 was to be Carter's tournament. He performed impeccably throughout the group stages and in the tense semi-final against South Africa he was resilient.

As well as graceful distribution, Carter was still known for the occasional midfield dash through the centre of defence, although these were seen less frequently in 2015 than against the Lions in 2005. Most tellingly, in the final Carter racked up the highest tackle count on the pitch, having the game of his life, and yet the whole time it seemed effortless.

The control that Carter exerted on a game was unrivalled. For an unpredictable fly-half who produces the moments of genius, it can be hard to remain consistent, but this was not the case for Carter, who used his instinct to push his opponent to exhaustion. Many fly-halves blessed with great tactical awareness tend to stand deeper than Carter, assessing their next move, allowing for the time to make a decision. This makes it hard to gain rhythm. Carter, by contrast, would take the ball on an almost flat line, keeping the ball in perpetual motion. Against Australia that day the attack was constant, and yet Carter always seemed to have enough time and space to make the right decision. With his head up and concentrating on his distribution so close to the gain line, he was met with Sekope Kepu, who made Carter's life difficult, but he dealt with the punishment.

Even all of these skills combined only tell a part of the story, as, like all greats, Carter played with a real fire for the big occasion. That 2015 final displayed this perfectly. After the stunning drop-goal Carter made sure he kept going to really put the boot in to his opponents. Receiving the ball on the restart, Carter put a little chip over the Wallabies defence, chasing it with venom to make a vicious and perfectly timed tackle on Kurtley Beale, which led to a New Zealand scrum and, only moments later, a penalty. Carter then kicked an uncharacteristically long goal kick, from 51m out, taking the points difference to ten points, demoralising the Australians completely.

And while it's true that Carter played for a great New Zealand team, surrounded by unusually talented players even by All Blacks standards, he stood out as a genius even among that wonder generation. Carter was a natural winner and there were no weaknesses to his game. There may be some goal-kickers who can reach greater distances from the tee, and some who can drive a shoulder into an opponent and drive him further back than Carter, but there are none who could have the overall impact on the game. There is no comparing the likes of Barry John to Jonny Wilkinson – they are so different. Carter is perhaps a mixture of both, with some Lynagh, Mehrtens and Larkham thrown in there. But crucially, Carter is unique. He doesn't mimic the greats, he eclipses them, and his enduring ability to surprise went right to his last game.

It was fitting, then, that with Dan Carter's final kick of the ball in international rugby, he was able to do something that he had never before done in a test. Kicking the final conversion with his right (wrong) foot was not arrogance, or the gloating act of a champion, but a genius allowing himself a rare moment of indulgence. It was for all of these reasons that, only a week later, he joined Richie McCaw as the only other player to be awarded three IRB Player of the Year awards, cementing his place as the greatest fly-half ever to play the sport.

6. MICHAEL JONES

Flanker, Western Samoa 1986, New Zealand 1987–98

When he was fit and willing, Auckland-born Michael Jones was a flawless and complete openside flanker, revolutionising the position with ruthless instinct, immaculate technique in the breakdown and a superior physique – just don't ask him to play on a Sunday.

As a staunchly religious man, Jones refused to play on Sundays, ruling him out of some crucial clashes, notably during the 1991 World Cup. The latter part of his career was also blighted by injury. It is perhaps for these reasons that Michael Jones is the least recognisable name in this top ten. A real joy to watch, Jones was a true inspiration when available, exuding charisma and confidence by the bucketload.

Despite the many setbacks, he was referred to as the 'almost perfect rugby player' by the legendary John Hart, his former All Blacks coach. He was respected by his peers and rivals and was a stoic and stirring captain.

Unusually, Jones made his debut for Western Samoa in 1986, aged twenty. This was to be his only appearance for the nation of his heritage. Eligibility rules were not as strict at that time and he was able to make his debut for the All Blacks a year later.

In the early part of his career, his blistering speed made him almost impossible to defend against. He had a mighty tackle and, in true All Blacks style, outstanding handling ability. He wasn't the tallest forward in the lineout, but was a formidable force as he could leap and spring above his opponents, an excellent jumper and a solid performer.

His first outing for the All Blacks was in the opening game of the inaugural World Cup, where he scored the initial try in their demolition job of Italy. Jones went on to play a major part in the World Cup campaign as New Zealand strolled their way to the title. As a bruising forward with the attacking vision of a centre, he came to epitomise the proud All Blacks style of rugby. Jones was involved in almost every important passage of play throughout the competition, scoring and setting up tries, spotting running lines and exploiting defensive weaknesses, turning the ball over and withstanding periods of defensive pressure with solidity. At

such a young age, Michael Jones gave a gifted and complete display, garnering universal acclaim.

This form continued for Jones through two more international seasons of unbeaten rugby for New Zealand, but much to Jones' disappointment, and that of spectators worldwide, he suffered a severe knee injury against Argentina in 1989, which ruled him out for a full year. His rehabilitation was slow and gruelling, but Jones fought his way back and his form steadily returned in time for selection for the 1991 World Cup. This time it was his religious beliefs and unfortunate fixture scheduling that stood in the way of his sporting success, as he was unavailable for three matches. He was impressive when he played, scoring a try against England in the opening game. Despite pressure to play, Jones was steadfast in his beliefs, which was respected by his teammates and coaches although it was to be to the detriment of the side, who did not look the same in his absence and were ultimately defeated 16-6 by Australia in the semi-final, with Jones watching from the stands.

His coaches understood that Jones' beliefs were important to him. His father had died when he was four and his mother had brought him up with the church as a large part of their lives. Jones had always devoted Sundays to his faith and that was never to change.

His conviction came under further pressure on the 1992 tour to Australia. The All Blacks had narrowly lost the first test by one point, with injuries to many key forwards in the process. The second test was on a Sunday, but still Jones refused to play and once again watched his team lose an important game from the sidelines. Although he returned for the final consolation victory six days later, it was starting to become a huge problem in a side that needed consistency as well as world-class players.

More injuries – a broken jaw in 1993 – and the Sunday situation saw Jones make only sporadic appearances for the All Blacks in the intervening years between World Cups. On occasions when he played he still demonstrated his world-class qualities, yet he seemed to suffer from the inconsistency in selection and indeed he did not go to the 1995 World Cup in South Africa as, like in 1991, the quarter- and semi-finals were scheduled for Sundays. Many believed that this was to be the end of his All Blacks career, that one which had started so prominently was perhaps going to fizzle out, allowing only a glimpse of his genius.

But in 1996 Jones reinvented his game and moved to the blind side; though he had lost the edge to his speed after his injuries, he developed the more physical side to his game. His commitment and tenacity paid dividends as he had somewhat of a resurgence, leading the wounded New Zealand in one of their most remarkable years as they recovered from the 1995 final defeat.

While wearing the number 6 Jones was instrumental in the All Blacks' furious pack as they recorded a record 43-6 win over their neighbours Australia before winning the inaugural Tri-Nations title and, most notably, winning a test series against the Springboks for the first time ever on South African soil.

But for all of Jones' mental strength, by 1998 many of the stars of that generation were starting to fade physically. Along with Zinzan Brooke, Wayne Shelford and Sean Fitzpatrick, the injuries and physicality of his game were taking their toll. Michael Jones retired that year, aged 33.

Jones retired with only 55 caps. In another time that would have been a sizeable number – it is the same as Colin Meads, for example. But as the number of games increased, the telling comparison is with contemporary hero Sean

Fitzpatrick, who managed almost double the level of test appearances. With a more consistent run in the side, free from injuries and a kinder fixture schedule, perhaps Michael Jones could have retired the greatest player of all time.

5. MARTIN JOHNSON

Lock, England 1993–2003

A legendary lock for both club and country, few players have embodied the role of captain as completely as Martin 'Johnno' Johnson.

On the domestic stage he played all his professional club rugby for Leicester Tigers, making his debut in 1989 before hanging up his boots a staggering sixteen years later, by which time they were established as the most successful club in England. His greatest achievement at this level was guiding the Tigers to back-to-back Heineken Cup victories, but there were also five league trophies, including a remarkable four in a row.

However, it is for his exploits on the international stage that he warrants his place at number five in this list. A giant of a man, there are few that compare to him in stature, both physically and as an imposing presence mentally for all those who opposed him. It does seem that Johnson shares many common features with the list of great captains. There are many who are lock forwards; many are colossal physical leaders who are consistent and strong at breakdowns, impenetrable in the scrum and vultures at the lineouts. The most immediate and obvious comparison to make with a captain of old is with All Blacks legend Colin 'Pinetree' Meads.

It was, in fact, Meads who saw the potential in Johnson from an early age, inviting the raw but promising teenager to New Zealand to play for King Country. Johnson played there for two seasons and even earned a call-up to play for New Zealand Under-21s.

He returned to Leicester in 1990 but did not make his international debut until 1993. Thrust into the England starting line-up as a late replacement for Wade Dooley, he had little time to prepare for international rugby. His influence was immediately appreciated and he was subsequently called up for the 1993 Lions tour to New Zealand – once again as a late replacement for Dooley, who had retired from the game at short notice. Johnson featured in two tests on that tour, after which he became a regular fixture for England.

England were the first to shine as the sport became professional and at this time were dominating the northern hemisphere with a Five Nations grand slam in 1995 and another Five Nations title in 1996. Even during the World Cup of 1995, it took the might of Jonah Lomu to end England's involvement in the competition and Martin Johnson was at the heart of England's relative success.

But following the retirement of Will Carling, England were lacking a captain. Phil de Glanville was given the title, and although he was a solid leader, he was not selected on the Lions tour after losing his place to a previously uncapped Will Greenwood – who soon usurped the captain at centre for England.

Martin Johnson's leadership potential was recognised by Lions coach Ian McGeechan, who decided that Johnson was the man to lead the tourists to the home of the world champions, South Africa. Once again, Johnno took the

unexpected pressure in his stride and led the Lions to an historic 2-1 victory. Johnson was well on his way to becoming one of the great leaders.

But Johnson did not lead that Lions tour alone and, in fact, Clive Woodward decided to award Lawrence Dallaglio the England captaincy. Both players thrived, despite the competition, and Johnson's influence was invaluable to the team. But following Lawrence Dallaglio's brush with the tabloids in 1999, Johnson was given the captaincy of England to relieve the pressure. Dallaglio remained in the team and together the duo would lead England through their most successful period ever.

Following two more Six Nations titles in 2000 and 2001, Johnson was selected to lead the Lions in their tour of Australia. A second tour as captain is an achievement which has never been matched.

It was 2003 that proved to be the pivotal year not only in Johnson's career but in the history of English rugby, with the inspirational lock leading from the front. First came a Six Nations grand slam, sealed in a dramatic and controversial fashion in a thumping 42-6 victory over Ireland at Lansdowne Road.

If we set aside tribal allegiances for one moment and try to think of the 2003 Lansdowne Road incident objectively as a piece of sport psychology, here were two great rivals: Ireland were themselves on the brink of a first grand slam in 55 years and they had the home advantage. Johnson managed to turn that advantage against Ireland by breaking protocol ahead of the anthems and lining England up on the right-hand side of the carpet, the traditional side for the home team. This managed to upset the Irish boys who lined up alongside them, leaving the left side of the carpet bare and forcing Irish President Mary McAleese to walk across the muddy pitch. Needless to say this caused a lot of boos to erupt from the stands and as officials asked Johnno to move, he refused point blank and gave each official a very angry talking-to.

Now, this clearly upset a lot of Irish fans and indeed many neutral supporters thought this was churlish and a real lack of sportsmanship, but with that wonderful power of hindsight, was it perhaps Johnson showing his insight into the winning psychology? All responsibility for the incident was purely on Johnson, who was more than capable of carrying it, leaving his players worry-free, but there were several members of that Irish squad who were clearly unsettled by the antics and their minds were less focused. The control was taken from them in a crucial moment.

There's something that all young players are taught: that if you really chase the first kick, set your stall out early with a big tackle, you can get inside their heads and show them you're tough and you're in control. Well, Johnson set his stall out before the ball was even kicked – between two world-class teams, it's moments like that which win games.

It has to be said that Johnson remained quiet over the incident for many years, but has since gone on to say that he had no prior knowledge of the protocol and only refused to move as the request did not come from the referee but instead from 'some guy' who, in Johnson's view, was less than polite about it.

In the immediate build-up to the 2003 World Cup, England raced up the world rankings by recording back-to-back victories against both New Zealand and Australia in a tour of the southern hemisphere, meaning that England entered the World Cup in Australia later that year as joint favourites with New Zealand. Not long afterwards, Johnson became the first Englishman to lift the Webb Ellis Cup.

It was a decade of Johnson performing at the top of his game for England that resulted in that World Cup win in 2003. It is testament to Johnson that since his retirement England have struggled to maintain any consistent form on the international stage, and while it's true that they reached another World Cup final and won a few Six Nations championships, England have never enjoyed the level of success and world domination that they did under Martin Johnson.

There are a few World Cup-winning captains and players in this list; in fact there are several representatives of that 2003 England team. Wilkinson made the last-gasp kick, Robinson scored the all-important try. What lifts Johnson above both of these men (as well as Robinson, Leonard, Dallaglio and Hill)? Martin Johnson retired after the World Cup and has said since that people suggested to him that perhaps he should have played his last game at Twickenham, or made it to a certain milestone with regards to caps. In his own words, 'If you're there for your own personal reasons … personal glories, then you should get out.'

While he began his career before the dawn of the professional era, his playing style was a throwback to a bygone era. A hard-nosed, no-nonsense forward with an uncompromising approach, Johnson won all there was to win – except for individual honours. He did not score often, in fact he retired with only two international tries in 92 test matches, but he was a winner through and through.

John Eales said of Johnno that in his presence other players around him played better, you could tell when a team had Martin Johnson in it because of the intensity and focus with which they played. Respected as one of the toughest men in the world of rugby, Johnson was a strong believer (along with coach Clive Woodward) that the direct and most obvious route was the best, and as such England were often criticised for playing a less than attractive style of rugby; but he proved that winning games was not about glitter.

There were men who could run faster, had greater technical ability, even a few who were stronger, but there was an implacable quality that Johnson brought that is harder to articulate, a quality that made him and the side he played in outstanding. What is also true is that Johnson's ability to relieve pressure, and the impact this had on the mentality of the squad, was a key factor in enabling the stars to take centre stage. A true leader is one that allows others to shine. In a team with Wilkinson, Greenwood, Robinson and Dallaglio, Johnson escaped the glitz and the glamour while relieving some of the responsibility and allowing those stars to excel.

The same bloody-minded belligerence that Johnson demonstrated time and time again on the pitch meant that he often did things that he didn't want his teammates to have to do. While endearing him to his own fans, this meant he was often less than popular with opposition supporters. The Irish incident aside, he was known to throw a punch or two and have some very strong words for referees that he disagreed with. On one or two occasions this was to the detriment of the team, but it was a fine line, and more often than not the protection he offered his team paid dividends.

Before 2003, and indeed since, the World Cup has only ever been won by nations from the southern hemisphere. South Africa, New Zealand and Australia have been dominant in the sport since the inaugural World Cup in 1987 with two World Cups apiece. The one player that England could not have done without in that landmark year was Martin Johnson.

4. BRIAN O'DRISCOLL

Centre, Ireland 1999–2014

By the time that Brian O'Driscoll retired from the sport of rugby union he was the most capped international player of all time. He was Ireland's greatest try scorer with 47, he was the first Irish captain to win a grand slam for 61 years, he led Ireland to four triple crowns, won Player of the Tournament at the Six Nations three times and remains the tournament's highest ever try scorer.

His emotional retirement in 2014 saw him bow out as not only the most famous Irish rugby player ever, but also the most respected and loved northern hemisphere player of the modern game. At number four in this list, Brian O'Driscoll is the greatest centre to ever play the game.

There have been a few players, Lomu and Wilkinson among them, whose acclaim and superstar status inspired kids across the world. O'Driscoll transcended the sport to become a household name and raise the profile of the entire sport internationally. Even US President Barack Obama namechecked Brian O'Driscoll's Ireland in a public speech ahead of their final Six Nations appearance. This was not the result of overnight success, of one particular event such as a last minute drop-goal that raised his profile to the presidential degree, but the result of over a decade of playing at the top level of the game.

In a similar fashion to Jonny Wilkinson's 1998 debut, and indeed only a few months later, O'Driscoll claimed his first full cap in an absolute 46-10 drubbing at the hands of the Australians in the first test of what was only Ireland's third ever tour Down Under. This was before he had even made a full senior appearance for his club, Leinster.

It did not knock his confidence, however, and the promising centre played in the World Cup of 1999 and scored his first try against the USA in the group stages. The potential was really starting to show, but he fully announced his arrival on the international scene during the inaugural Six Nations Championship of 2000, in what his captain Keith Wood described as 'the best performance by an Irish player I've ever seen'. O'Driscoll scored a hat-trick of tries against tournament favourites France to propel Ireland to their first win in Paris in 28 years.

Brian O'Driscoll's side-step was astonishing. He didn't have the David Campese goose-step or Shane Williams' bizarre and almost inhuman change in direction, but he could pull off a traditional waltzing side-step better than any player before or since. What's more, he had the tactical awareness to know exactly how and when to deploy it and the upper body strength to wade through a defender who was fortunate enough to get close to him. At the start of his career, he had blistering pace to complement this destructive power and against Australia in the 2001 Lions tour he demonstrated all of these abilities in one incredible individual try. His try-scoring record was outstanding, but it's worth bearing in mind the opportunities he made for others too; one of O'Driscoll's greatest strengths was in the offload. Phenomenal upper body strength in the tackle, coupled with the balance and presence of mind to find a teammate, meant that he was able to shift and change the pace of a game at the drop of a hat. That isn't to say he was all attack. A great centre also needs the defensive capabilities to smash the living daylights out of emerging back-row forwards making precious inches over the gain line. As

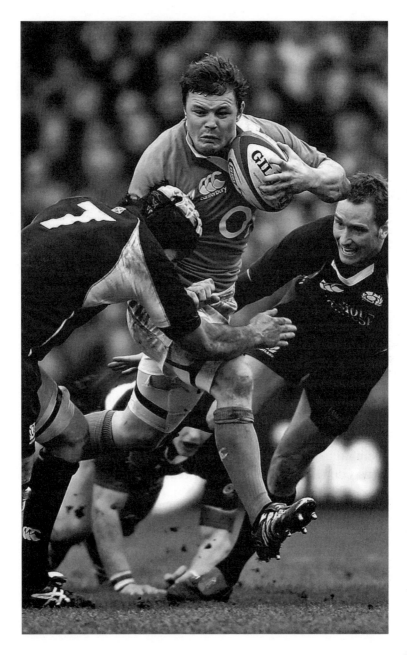

O'Driscoll's career progressed, as his pace dropped and his defence became more important to him and to Ireland, this is precisely the part of his game that improved.

One quality many great players have in common is selflessness. Time and time again players on this list of greats have been known for a lack of self-preservation, with careers consequently ravaged by injury. Brian O'Driscoll is no exception. But if there is a humility in this willingness to make sacrifices and put one's body on the line, it goes hand in hand with unwavering self-belief.

In 2004, Ireland managed to end England's 22-match winning streak at Twickenham. In a post-match interview an impassioned O'Driscoll referred to the 'so-called world champions in a so-called fortress'. Cue English media frenzy. But O'Driscoll seemed to toe the right side of the line that separates arrogance from self-belief. He went into every game expecting to win; this can-do attitude was a breath of fresh air and revitalised the entire Irish national team and fans.

O'Driscoll's self-belief was also apparent in the build-up to a Lions tour of New Zealand in 2005. At a time when many saw the All Blacks as virtually unbeatable (most teams therefore being beaten before the first ball was kicked), and rivals were lining up to pour praise on them, O'Driscoll declined to follow suit; instead, in all his media appearances he was doing what any real competitor would do and talking about the win.

As it was, he was denied, in the cruellest fashion, the opportunity to test himself against his illustrious opponents. His tour lasted approximately one minute after a double spear tackle from All Blacks Tana Umaga and Keven Mealamu. At the breakdown, after the ball had been played, O'Driscoll was lifted on to his head and was incredibly lucky not to have received life-changing injuries. Both of the New

Zealanders escaped punishment. O'Driscoll was out injured for seven months, following an operation on his dislocated shoulder.

With an injury like that, the psychological recovery can often take far longer. For a player who puts his body on the line to that extent, it can sometimes take a while to get that edge back. Not for Brian. Aside from the glittering mazy runs, appearing to walk on water over his opposition, O'Driscoll was able to inspire in his ability to rise up and withstand this level of punishment.

Inevitably for someone with this level of career spanning over a decade, injuries started to take their toll on O'Driscoll. He missed the 2007 World Cup entirely, and between intermittent niggles it looked possible that his career could be on the decline. But his mentality and resolve remained and he continued to be a match-winner. It's true that he may not quite have had the legs to make as much impact with the dizzying and awe-inspiring runs of old – though that's not to say he wasn't still world-class with ball in hand – but he developed into a different player. His defensive game improved drastically as he adapted to become somewhat of an auxiliary back-row forward, winning crucial turnover ball at the breakdown and controlling a game from a much tighter position.

Even though his passing wasn't quite perfect and his kicking out of hand was not something he was known for, he retained his reputation as a magician with a bag of footballing trick shots. There were countless occasions where he amazed spectators, opposition and his own teammates. One that springs to mind came when playing for his club Leinster against Wasps in the Heineken Cup. A chip and chase didn't quite go his way so he got underneath the bounce with another kick, chased and caught that one for a dazzling try. There is even footage from training that shows him chase a high kick only to control it with his feet and catch the resulting bounce. This level of improvisation and uncoachable audacity is part of what made him so legendary.

But it was 2009 that was perhaps O'Driscoll's annus mirabilis, as he led Ireland to a Six Nations grand slam, only the second in their history. He scored in all of the matches bar one and was named as Player of the Tournament. That same year, he led Leinster to their first Heineken Cup victory and was selected for his third British & Irish Lions tour.

This was no swansong. O'Driscoll's 100th cap beckoned in 2010 and although the niggles continued and Ireland struggled to continue their outstanding form, he did lead Ireland into the quarter-finals of the 2011 World Cup. But surgery in the aftermath of the tournament subsequently ruled him out of the 2012 Six Nations. It's true that the injuries were becoming more debilitating and frequent, but O'Driscoll adapted further still, and when fit was just as influential for Ireland as when he first found form a decade earlier. Many young centres lined up hoping to make a name for themselves by physically overpowering the Irish hero, and just as many were humiliated and educated in return.

There was one last opportunity for a now 34-year-old O'Driscoll to add a victorious British & Irish Lions tour to his collection as he was picked for a remarkable fourth and final tour. Despite a wealth of talent from across the home nations, most notably in the form of Wales' Jamie Roberts. O'Driscoll was selected ahead of the outstanding Wales midfielder for the first two tests, but was controversially dropped for the series decider, with Roberts coming into the side and scoring an all-important try. The fact that decision was seen as controversial is testament to the influence O'Driscoll continued to have on a team.

Even though his desire to win was paramount and he was always a true competitor, O'Driscoll's crowd-pleasing nature often shone through. He was known to astonish crowds with a pass between the legs, and a no-look, around-the-back offload to Johnny Sexton for Leinster is one that many watched on repeat and became a YouTube favourite.

O'Driscoll relished the spotlight: a man-of-the-match performance against Italy in his final Six Nations Championship in 2014 when he surpassed the record for the most capped player of all time showed that he was always able to find another gear when the pressure was on. This was Brian O'Driscoll, a fearsome warrior who struck fear into his opponents, but did so with a smile on his face.

3. DAVID CAMPESE

Wing/full-back, Australia 1982–96

Rugby union is not a sport for individuals. Rarely when we talk about greatness do we talk about a single player in a game, with little regard for the team around him. David Campese played alongside some wonderful players but even alone he was a player who had the magic to draw the neutral and indifferent spectator in. He was a player who had the speed and athleticism, but most importantly the character, to lift an entire team.

That team was Australia, and Campese was the star player of their resurgence in the 1980s. For a long time, he held the world record for the most international tries scored, a record only bettered by Daisuke Ohata of Japan, who overtook him in 2006. David 'too easy' Campese is an outspoken national hero of Australia and the most galvanising and viscerally exciting rugby union player of all time.

In order to accommodate Roger Gould, Campese played a surprising number of tests at full-back, including during the 1987 World Cup, but it was on the wing where he kept crowds tingling with anticipation and where his mercurial talent was best displayed.

Strong and fast, Campese had an excellent sturdy frame with ball in hand and was incredibly difficult to stop. He is probably the best attacking player ever, and on paper had no real defensive weakness. A solid and reliable tackler, 'Campo' was dependable under the pressure of the high ball and possessed a strong tactical boot to match. Campese's brash and arrogant style polarised supporters and sometimes distracted from his talent. But this superiority both on and off the pitch was justified, and it only frustrated his opponents more when he was able to back up his strong words with impeccable play.

Campese didn't just let his rugby do the talking and he managed to get under the skin of the All Blacks even before his debut. When asked about facing the great winger Stu Wilson, he responded to a journalist, 'Stu who?' Campese was never one to shy away from controversial comments, but on this occasion he had just switched codes from rugby league and claimed he genuinely didn't know who he was up against. Despite Australia losing the game, Campese impressed and outplayed his vastly more experienced opponent, scoring a wonderful try in the process. It was to be the world's first glimpse of his trademark 'goose-step'. Always different, never content with the standard way of doing things, Campese wasn't happy to simply side-step a defender; he perfected a far more baffling technique. A small hesitation, followed by a huge burst of perfectly timed pace just as the defender hesitated, leaving him flat-footed – and Campese would be gone. It has been attempted by many players since, but it takes a huge amount of skill to pull it off. Joe Rokocoko and Shane Williams had their own variations, but David Campese made the move his own.

Campese may have only been 22 years old when he first toured Britain and Ireland, the first time he faced any of the home nations' sides, but he was far from raw. Having already enjoyed test victories over New Zealand, he had faced tougher opposition and was full of confidence. As were the home nations. In the previous two tours (in 1975–76 and 1981–82) Australia had only managed to beat Ireland and were arriving as underdogs. But with a side that contained Mark Ella, Nick Farr-Jones and Michael Lynagh as well as David Campese, the home nations were in for a shock as Australia completed a grand slam. Campese was granted real freedom playing on the wing outside that incredibly creative back line. His most memorable moment came in the final match of the tour, when Australia beat the Barbarians 37-30 and Campese ran from inside his own half, turning the Welsh centre Robert Ackerman inside out. Ackerman was a sound defender, but Campese had him isolated, forcing him to backtrack a huge distance. Campese then put Michael Hawker in to finish the move off. Australia truly announced themselves on the world stage in that tour and proved they were a force to be reckoned with, blessed with talent that was only just emerging.

The Wallabies went from strength to strength in Campese's early years. Even after the retirement of Ella, Campese's magic was still there to be seen; indeed, he matured into an even more accomplished player. He was utterly immeasurable in Australia's series victory over the All Blacks in 1986. It

was the first time they had won the Bledisloe Cup on New Zealand soil since 1949 and as a consequence they entered the inaugural 1987 World Cup as the favourites.

Ultimately though, it was not to be, as Serge Blanco and his French side hit their peak – in a knockout tournament, there is little to be done against Les Bleus on their day. It was disappointing for Australia and they entered something of a slump in the following years. The Wallabies looked lost and Campese's form suffered. Heavy defeats in the Bledisloe Cup and the rise of John Kirwan for the All Blacks affected his confidence. Campese was a showman, something he had demonstrated time and time again, not least in that famous sparkling run against Ackerman for the Barbarians, and it seemed in those barren years that his desire to show off was getting the better of him. This frustration manifested itself completely in the decisive third test against the touring British & Irish Lions in 1989.

Even throughout these trying times for Australia, Campese was still scoring tries. He scored six tries in three games against England, Scotland and Italy in the winter before the Lions tour, and it was certainly not through their brilliant backs that they were losing games. As the Lions approached, there was an indication that the Wallabies had sorted their tactics out. Michael Lynagh's excellent tactical kicking and Australia's relentless chasing kept the Lions out of the first test entirely and the Wallabies won comfortably by an eighteen-point margin. Contrasting with Australia's approach, a physical and violent second test followed, which the Lions won, setting the stage for a series decider in Sydney. Campese had been a comparatively peripheral figure throughout the series by his excellent standards and hit the self-destruct button somewhat as a horrendously wayward pass in a dangerous area led to an easy try for Ieuan

Evans in the corner and Australia lost the game 19-18. Had the pass made it to Wallabies full-back Greg Martin, it would most likely have led to a devastating counter-attack and Campese would have been a hero. Instead, he was derided, shouldering the blame for his nation's failure (and the area of the pitch where the incident occurred is now known as 'Campo's Corner').

Campese was always unpredictable; this was a part of what made his attacking brilliance so unique. But on this one occasion, a painful mistake cost his team the series. Campo's head didn't drop. A competitive desire for redemption and an urge to show off drove Campese onward as he developed a thick skin and grew into the form of his career.

Australia bounced back and developed momentum going into the 1991 World Cup, and this was to be Campese's year. Utterly superb throughout the tournament, he was never more brilliant than against reigning champions New Zealand in the semi-final. His tribulations in previous years gave him a mental edge as he decided not to face the Haka; somewhat disrespectfully, he practised his goal-kicking instead. This served as an effective distraction and the tactic had the desired effect as Campese scored a ludicrous individual try very early in the game. There was a huge amount of audacity in receiving the ball as first receiver on the All Blacks' 22 and running an almost sideways line despite an overlap existing. This unexpected movement really threw the New Zealand defence and as they hesitated, Campese sprinted and found himself over the try line in the corner. If the wonder try he scored was a moment of brilliance, then the one he set up was pure genius. Scooping up a loose ball that dropped nicely for him on the bounce, Campese drew in the defence and offloaded to Tim Horan, blindly, over his shoulder. This was not a panic throw, it was calm and decisive and Campese had been able to predict Horan's run seconds earlier, it was hailed as a 'miracle pass'.

Campese was a player with bags of flair, one who played beautiful rugby for the spectators. Australia's final opponents in that World Cup were to be England, who played a style that was the anti-Campese. They had defeated Scotland without scoring a try and were more about building a solid base from their forwards and winning with the boot than making dazzling runs and exciting fans. Campese started with the mind games again, stating that he could never play for England, but alluding that if he did he would have to play at fly-half, just so he could get a touch of the ball. He went on to call England's style of play boring and ruinous to the image of the sport. Once again, the mind games worked as England appeared all out of sorts, running with the ball more often and running into trouble. Australia won 12-6 and Campese finished as Player of the Tournament, becoming a household name.

Campese played his rugby with an instinctive magic that lifted him high above his peers. A ripple of anticipation ran through a crowd when he was given the ball and ran with that unwavering self-belief that followed him off the pitch. Retiring in 1996 just as the sport was transitioning into professionalism, Campese's legacy is a shadow over Australian rugby. The Wallabies, inspired, continue to produce wonderful, free-flowing back lines, although no winger has quite been able to reproduce the delight of David Campese. Since retiring, he has not lost his ability to provide entertainment and controversy, and is always happy to oblige when a journalist needs a provocative remark about the state of English rugby.

2. RICHIE McCAW

Flanker, New Zealand 2001–15

With an international test win rate of nearly 90 per cent and a career spanning nearly fifteen years, Richie McCaw won thirteen Bledisloe Cups, ten Tri-Nations (or Rugby Championship) tournaments, three IRB Player of the Year awards and consecutive World Cups. He is the most capped international player ever and has won over 100 tests, a record which no other player looks likely to even come close to in the near future; and yet, even combined, these records only tell part of the Richie McCaw story. Sometimes vilified, but more often revered, McCaw is the greatest All Black of all time. This inspirational and highly competitive flanker has won unparalleled respect from his rugby peers and achieved everything he could have achieved as a player and as an inspirational leader.

McCaw's anticipation and phenomenal work rate make him the greatest forward the game has ever produced. Even against sides that can spread the ball, McCaw has been known to make several breakdowns in a row, relentlessly driving the opposition and frustrating them to the point of a turnover.

Playing flat-out and pushing the limit of the laws throughout his career, he has drawn criticism from many frustrated rivals who have seen McCaw confuse referees, who have consequently let a few questionable decisions pass over the years. But if you're not pushing the boundaries and on the edge of giving a penalty away as a back-row forward, then you're not doing your job properly. Many coaches,

pundits and rival players have accused McCaw of cheating, with technical foul play in the breakdown; however, often the accusations have led to discussion over the rules rather than any disciplinary action for McCaw. By sheer numbers, owing to the length of his career and his ability to make successive breakdowns, he has inevitably been given the benefit of the doubt on occasion, just as he has inevitably committed many offences. One figure that is hard to argue with, though, is that he only received two yellow cards in his career. His rate of conceding penalties was high, and McCaw always risked his relationship with referees, but he was smart enough not to get sent off and ultimately won matches, developing this formidable reputation and influence as his career progressed.

When McCaw made his debut in November 2001, it was somewhat of a fallow period for New Zealand (although admittedly, if such a thing can be said to exist, it is perhaps only in comparison to more recent years). Australia had won the last four Bledisloe Cups on the bounce for the only time in history and as world champions were overshadowing their rivals. The undisputed master of the breakdown was to make his All Blacks debut aged just twenty, against Ireland, playing on the blind side. In this game he displayed the strength and stature of a far more experienced defender, with that very Kiwi trait of having the speed and handling skills to match. He excelled, New Zealand won the game, and McCaw hit the ground running.

McCaw's arrival coincided with a reversal of fortunes for the All Blacks as they began their return to their comfortable position as the dominant force in world rugby. Tri-Nations triumphs in 2002 and 2003 saw them enter the World Cup with high hopes, but they were ultimately disappointed in the semi-final against the Wallabies. Despite the disappointment of this exit after arriving as favourites, McCaw's great performances were not the only shining light for New Zealand, as they also found the natural successor to Carlos Spencer in Dan Carter. Carter would be alongside McCaw in much of his success throughout his career, marshalling the backs in much the same way that McCaw leads the team, the tactician who would make the most of the possession and domination that McCaw granted him.

The first time McCaw led his country was in 2004, aged just 23. His career went from strength to strength after this, switching to the openside role in 2005 to help see off the British & Irish Lions. The two stars of that particular series were the indelible combination of Dan Carter and Richie McCaw, together giving a generation of All Blacks immense hope for the future. That year saw the first of four successive Tri-Nations championships as Dan Carter was named IRB Player of the Year in 2005, with McCaw winning a year later after being named permanent captain following the retirement of Tana Umaga. In fact, over the next eleven seasons, six of the IRB awards would go to either Carter or McCaw, with three each – just one further example of their combined dominance.

McCaw was not the most agile or athletic back-row forward to play the game, but his determination, technique and preparation propelled him to the top and his physical endurance kept him there. McCaw led his team by example. He became famous for making extensive notes and for his pre-match preparation in which he would rehearse every scenario and create game plans for any eventuality. Imagining every breakdown in meticulous detail, McCaw used his increasing experience to constantly improve not only his own performance, but that of every player to play alongside him. With that hugely impressive and frankly outrageous win rate in mind, the only minor blips on McCaw's record are the 2007 World Cup and a difficult aftermath that included three defeats to the Springboks in 2009. That said, there have been trying occasions when McCaw has led New Zealand back from the brink of defeat with unshakable self-belief, something which, as the leader, he instilled into his entire team.

Although he finished as the star player in the 2011 World Cup campaign, McCaw had struggled to make fitness as a stress fracture in his right foot severely hindered his preparation, and indeed the injury resurfaced during the group stages. But he recovered in time to be at the heart of everything the All Blacks did as they redeemed the failures of 2007 with a 20-6 semi-final victory over Australia, followed by a horrifically tense 8-7 victory over their bogey team France in the final. This accomplishment was all the more remarkable as it was achieved without Dan Carter, meaning the reliance on McCaw's strength of character was all the more prominent. That said, the entire squad gave some incredible performances and it was starting to look like the All Blacks had assembled one of the greatest sides ever, leading not just from beautiful free-flowing attack, but accompanied by a solid and robust defensive line.

McCaw demonstrated his greatness no better than when in defence. Just one example of this was in the 2007 Bledisloe Cup when Mark Gerrard looked set to make the corner after a Wallabies breakthrough. McCaw tracked all the way back, anticipating the run. He was not only able to make a try-saving tackle, but in one swift movement he stripped the ball back from the suddenly isolated winger in a matter of moments, completely destroying the attack and putting New Zealand back on the front foot. Of course, Dan Carter was on hand to kick his side to victory that day, but Australia lost much of their attacking potency due to the All Blacks captain McCaw. This was not consistency was McCaw's greatest power and not a game went by where he didn't make the opposition weaker in exactly this way.

The 2015 World Cup saw New Zealand enter the competition looking likely to be the first side to retain the title. The stage was set, the sleepy hosts England knocked out in the group stages by a savage and exciting Australia side. The Wallabies had looked to be in a shambles only a year before and had had a less than ideal preparation leading up to the World Cup, although they now looked completely revitalised thanks to their excellent coach Michael Cheika. This was to be an exciting World Cup, dominated by the southern hemisphere sides and eye-catching back-row performances. With the likes of Michael Hooper and David Pocock dominating the headlines for turnovers won, questions were quietly being asked of Richie McCaw's disciplinary record and whether or not the All Blacks were sleepwalking through the group stages. Many of these questions were asked by people who underestimated Argentina's refreshing play and how easily New Zealand had dismissed them in their opening game. Those dissenting voices fell silent by the time the All Blacks destroyed France in a 62-13 victory in a record-breaking result for a World Cup quarter-final. It was an inspired performance from the entire squad against a less than impressive French side, far from their best.

A much tougher test of character came against South Africa in a physical semi-final in which New Zealand found themselves with their backs to the wall and only a Dan Carter drop-goal separated the sides as the game finished 20-18. A spirited South African side were knocking on the door of the All Blacks defence for huge periods of the game, particularly when the sublime Jerome Kaino had a momentary lapse in judgement to find himself in the sin bin and New Zealand were reduced to fourteen men. New Zealand were far from their best, but they won through immense mental strength. They did not falter, or fall apart, but were led by McCaw, who rose to the challenge and resolutely saw off the Springboks to set up the historic final against the Wallabies.

New Zealand faced a strong Australian side, who probably could have won the World Cup had they been playing against any other side in history, but not against Richie McCaw's All Blacks. Right from the kick-off, there was only going to be one winner. It only truly looked like a contest in ten minutes of Aussie revival when once again New Zealand found themselves down to fourteen men, but the day belonged to Ma'a Nonu, Conrad Smith, Keven Mealamu, to Dan Carter and to McCaw – the special generation of All Blacks who collectively made the greatest sporting side in history, led by the great Richie McCaw.

1. GARETH EDWARDS

Scrum-half, Wales 1967–78

To discuss the legendary status of Sir Gareth Edwards, we have to begin with 'that try'. Strange that for many fans of a certain age or nostalgic persuasion, the Barbarians game of 1973, a game which was not a capped test but an end-of-tour exhibition event, goes down as the example of the pinnacle of rugby union. The wealth of talent on display was staggering. In an era which supplied more stars than any other, that day saw many of them on the pitch at once. Many had played in the victorious Lions tour of '71. With Phil Bennett in place of the now retired Barry John, the Baa-Baas set out to repeat their famous demolition of the All Blacks, but crucially, the pressure was off. Although both sides set out to win, they also set out to entertain. They were there to pass, run, and play free-flowing rugby, and to showcase their talent in front of the world.

It's only fitting then, that on this day, the greatest player of all time, in what was regarded as the greatest game of all time, scored the greatest try ever recorded. It was so good, in fact, that it is known as simply 'that try'. A certain inflection in the voice when naming 'that try' has the power to evoke a whole other era, one where Wales reigned supreme over the world and one phase of play can carry more drama than most games can in 80 minutes.

It was an incredible spectacle, with the tone set by Edwards' try in the opening minutes. It was Phil Bennett who started the move, receiving the ball deep in his own half, side-stepping three players and running sideways across the line (in a sight that would make modern-day coaches panic). He evaded the chasing Kiwis and passed the ball to J.P.R. Williams, who fed the ball down the line with slick handling between five more players before finding Edwards, who had popped up out on the wing. There was still 30 yards to go, but Edwards applied the gas, racing down the touchline, leaving defenders in his wake and finishing with a dive past the full-back into the corner. A try that leaves you panting no matter how many times you watch the replay.

The rest of the game continued in this beautiful, free-flowing fashion. There are many who grew up in the 1960s and '70s who believe that the modern game pales in

comparison, perceiving that the ultra-defensive way teams set up now rarely allows for a game such as Barbarians v. New Zealand in 1973. When reliving these moments through the archives, it's difficult to argue with that logic – although it should be recognised that very few games of any era live up to that one. That game lives on as a unique spectacle.

It's difficult to compare generations, and yet, irrefutably, Edwards would have been great in whatever era he played. He adapted to the rugby around him, he responded with such impeccable instinct that you almost feel that the more drilled and practised the modern-day professionals are, the more the instinct-led Edwards would be able to exploit that as weakness. A proud Welshman, Edwards' revelled in the praise heaped upon him from his supporters.

The two countries with the proudest rugby tradition, where the sport is the most revered and where it unquestionably reigns supreme, are New Zealand and Wales. With Edwards being a Welshman, it is perhaps even more special that his greatest moments came against the toughest of opponents – New Zealand. In this sport of fierce rivalries, a player can be revered by one nation and reviled in another – take Martin Johnson, Richie McCaw and David Campese, for example. One can create regional heat maps where citing those as greats will be met with derision or admiration. One of the only players whose legacy is felt worldwide is Gareth Edwards.

Edwards' career coincided with the golden age of Welsh rugby. Never before or since had they been quite so prolific. They produced an entire team full of stars, at the centre of which was Edwards. He combined pace, strength and intelligence to devastating effect. His perfect technique gave him a strong kicking game and incredible passing ability, and he was tactically astute both in defence and attack. He was a superlative athlete of the highest skills, the complete package as a rugby player. Put simply, he was the ultimate scrum-half.

He played his first game for Wales in 1967, aged nineteen, against France at the Parc des Princes in Paris. Wales lost that match 20-14, but consistent success was just around the corner. Wales were on the verge of collective greatness, and their curve of success correlates exactly with that of Edwards, the man who personifies that era better than any.

Of course, Edwards and Wales were to go on to complete dominance of the Five Nations throughout his career, winning seven titles and three grand slams. And although Mervyn Davies was a more regular captain when Edwards broke through, it's clear that Edwards was always Wales' big hope. He remains the youngest player ever to have captained Wales, a record he set in 1968 against Scotland, when he was just twenty years old.

It was not until 1969, when Edwards founded his partnership with Barry John (see page 143), that Wales really found their feet. In the early part of his career, this combination helped propel the fledgling scrum-half on the path to greatness. With stability outside him, Edwards was able to truly showcase his ability. Although able to score wonderful individual tries, he needed a world-class outside half to be on the receiving end of his graceful passes. John was able to step up and complemented Edwards' abilities well.

Although Barry John was still learning his craft, they won the Five Nations in their first full year of partnership with Wales in 1969, and it would have been a grand slam if not for an 8-8 draw with France. They finished as unbeaten champions, and although there was no grand slam at the end of it, in their final game they managed to destroy England 30-9 in front of a jubilant home crowd.

It was not long before Wales were able to achieve that coveted grand slam, their first in nearly twenty years. The 1971 Five Nations was the first time the world really saw the potential of the lethal half-back pairing of Barry John and Gareth Edwards, as they set the championship alight in two incredibly comfortable home wins over England and Ireland and two hard-fought away wins against France and, in particular, Scotland. In that final game, Wales left it to the last minute to secure victory by a single point with a last-gasp conversion scored by flanker John Taylor. Both Barry John and Gareth Edwards scored tries that day and that titanic tussle was a foretaste of the successes to come.

The next two years saw bizarre interruptions to that success in unusual years for the Five Nations Championship. In 1973, all five teams finished level on points, sharing the championship equally for the only time in history. The year before the championship had been left incomplete, with neither Scotland nor Wales wishing to travel to Dublin as the Troubles were flaring up, leaving Wales at the top of the resulting table with three games played and three comprehensive victories. It was in this year that Edwards scored one of the greatest solo tries ever caught on film. After an opportunistic take at the bottom of a ruck following a stolen Scottish lineout, Edwards spotted a gap inside his own half and bolted. Finding himself closed down, he performed a perfect kick and chase, chipping the ball over the Scottish full-back and touching down in the corner.

Edwards had a blistering turn of pace that kept him away from the biggest impact hits. Due to his size, he was more prone to wriggle through gaps rather than crash through a defence. Edwards was the creative spark who initiated everything: at the heart of every move, at the foot of every ruck, dictating play.

Playing in a team full of stars certainly allowed us to really witness the significance of Edwards; the enormity of his talent was brought out by those closest to him, namely Barry John (and later Phil Bennett) at fly-half and Mervyn Davies at number eight. But in those years the entire back line of Wales was full of talent with the likes of J.P.R. Williams, J.J. Williams and Gerald Davies. Meanwhile, Lions teammates included Willie John McBride, Andy Irvine, Gordon Brown and Mike Gibson. Again, it was a formidable line-up even without Edwards, but the scrum-half outshone these luminaries and was the best of them. Together, they brought out the best in each other, resulting in an era of rugby that has never been repeated.

Wales' next grand slam was not to be until 1976, and by this time the great Barry John had retired, which would have been a devastating blow had Wales not had an almost ready-made replacement in Phil Bennett. Edwards and Bennett had masterminded a famous defeat of Australia in Cardiff in 1975 and entered the 1976 championship full of confidence. Only France had prevented them from a grand slam in '75, although Wales had claimed the title, and indeed it was France who were their toughest opposition in '76, being the only side who even came within ten points of the Welsh, in the final game in Cardiff.

France ruined the party the following year, with a grand slam of their own. But the Welsh were back on top the next year: Edwards finished his career against France in Cardiff in 1978, a game that they won 16-7. And Edwards won his third grand slam with it.

In addition to his 53 Wales caps, Edwards featured in ten test appearances for the British & Irish Lions, travelling on the 1968, 1971 and 1974 tours. Still learning his craft in '68, he featured in both a draw and a loss in two tests of a losing tour to South Africa. Edwards used this experience to enter into two Lions tours of legend. The first of these, to New Zealand, is still the only tour on which the Lions have emerged victorious against the mighty All Blacks. Edwards featured in all four test matches and was the architect of this success, playing magnificently throughout.

The third tour was arguably the greatest Lions tour ever. The tourists played 22 matches, unbeaten throughout. Their belief was unwavering: nobody would be able to beat them. And it was with brimming confidence that they were able to enter into the physical battle against the Springboks.

Edwards was a marked man, singled out as the most influential player, and word was out that some of the provincial sides were out to get a bit too physical with the star Lions. Whether or not the rumours were true, Captain Willie John McBride had a plan for this. Sure enough, Edwards was the victim of a late tackle and the infamous '99 call' was issued. The ensuing violence demonstrated the lengths that teams had to go to to keep Edwards quiet – as well as the lengths his teammates would go to to protect their star man and keep him fit enough to help them make history.

The most crucial attributes that any pack leader wants in his scrum-half are a natural instinct and unwavering confidence. Consistency is important too, but no matter how accurate he is, or fast, if he scoops the ball out ad infinitum and becomes predictable then a good opposition back row will destroy the outside half.

That's what made Gareth Edwards so special. He had all the traditional skills so the opposition couldn't take their eyes off him for a moment; as he proved time and time again, one lapse and he was through the gap and an entire game plan was undone. Having that threat created more room for his own back line because the opposition back row had to check for a split-second to see what Edwards might have up his sleeve.

Fundamentally, Edwards understood when to make breaks and when to pass, forming the blueprint for every scrum-half since. Edwards left a legacy that will be tough to match.

Also available

the
50

PETER
PUGH

MOST INFLUENTIAL
BRITONS
OF THE LAST 100 YEARS

ISBN: 9781785780349 (paperback) / 9781785780356 (ebook)

Also available

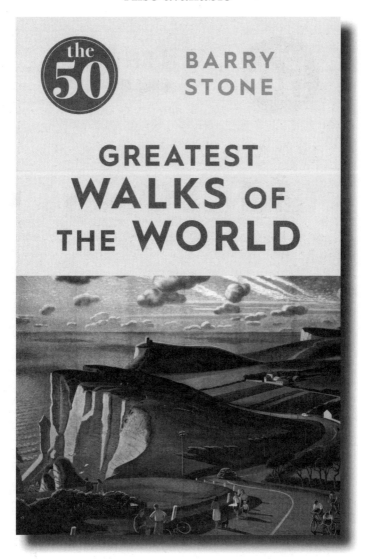

ISBN: 9781785780639 (paperback) / 9781785780646 (ebook)

Also available

the 50

ANTHONY
LAMBERT

GREATEST
TRAIN JOURNEYS
OF THE WORLD

ISBN: 9781785780653 (paperback) / 97817857880660 (ebook)

IN ASSOCIATION WITH
TIMPSON